# Vegan
# Desserts in jars

Adorably Delicious Pies, Cakes, Puddings and much more

Kris Holechek Peters

**Ulysses Press**

*In loving memory of Mary Troyan (1907–2013)*
*and Victoria Mikelonis (1910–2004)*

Published by:
Ulysses Press
P.O. Box 3440
Berkeley, CA 94703
www.ulyssespress.com

ISBN: 978-1-61243-225-0
Library of Congress Catalog Number 2013938636

Printed in the United States by Bang Printing

10 9 8 7 6 5 4 3 2 1

Acquisitions editor: Kelly Reed
Managing editor: Claire Chun
Editor: Lauren Harrison
Proofreader: Elyce Berrigan-Dunlop
Index: Sayre Van Young
Photography: © Kris Holechek
Design and layout: what!design @ whatweb.com

Distributed by Publishers Group West

# TABLE OF CONTENTS

# INTRODUCTION

Canning jars give me warm fuzzies. My great-grandmothers both canned, and their annual harvest was highly coveted in my family. As our family grew, it could sometimes get ugly in the competition to get a jar of Grandma M's pickled beets or Grandma T's pears. Canning jars are little vessels filled with love, love that keeps on giving as the jars are cycled through, year after year, batch after batch, making their way from home to home.

The great thing about the jars is their versatility. They certainly house canned items, but they are also the perfect receptacles for items you want to take on the go. I love using my favorite wide-mouth pint jar to tote along a breakfast smoothie or some iced coffee on my trek to work. A little 4-ounce jar is perfect for taking hummus for a snack, and an 8-ounce jar can carry yogurt and granola for breakfast. The uses go on and on.

But by far the most glorious use of the canning jar is for my most favorite of foods—dessert. The jars' portability makes them incredibly convenient, and a perfect, single-serving treat is a beautiful thing to present to loved ones. Even if you just want portion control, it's hard to not smile when cracking the top crust on a petite pie or scooping out a creamy mouthful of mousse. Whether you're serving a half-dozen to a table of dinner guests or presenting a sweet little jar to a coworker, each one truly does feel like a gift.

What makes these treats especially wonderful is that rather than buying some specialty dessert receptacle, the beloved canning jar can be repurposed in dozens of different ways between treats (however, it's not advised to have too much time between treats; it makes the jars quite sad and lonely).

This book is a product of my love affair with canning jar sweets, which began long ago when I first made the connection that the very same jars I submerged in my water-bath canner could also function in the oven. Amazing! It turned my baking world upside down and since then, nary a canning jar can be found in my house that doesn't contain an unexpected morsel of goodness within its glass walls.

So hold onto your jars, grab a spatula, and surprise your loved ones with some cute and resourceful treats that are sure to make them smile and say, "Nom!"

## KNOW YOUR JARS

Canning jars come in an array of shapes and sizes, but for the purposes of baking, smaller is better. You can assemble a nice variety by looking at your current stash and then picking up extra jars at thrift shops and estate sales, and by rooting around through your mother's possessions (oh wait, that might just be me). If you're starting from scratch, look in the baking section of your local grocery store or in your local hardware store. Canning jars are remarkably easy to come across.

**SIZING:** The smaller jars typically come in 4-ounce, 8-ounce (half-pint), and 16-ounce (pint) sizes. You will see all three used in this book, but mostly the 4- and 8-ounce varieties. For the 8-ounce size, a variety of the shorter, fatter jars and the taller, skinnier jars will provide more versatility.

**MOUTH OPENING:** There are two standard mouth sizes for jars: standard and wide-mouthed. This difference will apply particularly when deciding what type of treat you're making. If you'll be taking the treat out of the jar to serve it, you'll want a straight-sided jar. Otherwise, a jar with the mouth narrower than its body will work.

**LIDS AND RIMS:** Depending on what kind of treat you're making, you might want to cap it up. Lids can be reused when using jars for basic things like treats, but if you are using them to actually can—to seal and store food—always use new lids. They can be purchased for next to nothing and can be found at practically any grocery store (check in the baking section or by food storage products). Additionally, local hardware stores (like Ace) typically have impressive selections of canning goods. Rims can be reused indefinitely, as long as they are in good shape and aren't rusty.

*A note on jar safety:* When baking, be sure that you are using a proper canning jar; reusing jars from commercial food doesn't guarantee they are oven-safe. Additionally, always check for chips and cracks before baking. Be wary of baking in antique jars, as glass was tempered differently in the past; typically these are the kinds that have a blue tint and visible air bubbles in the glass. They are better suited for dry mixes and other kinds of non-heated gifts.

# THE PANTRY

Here are the recommended ingredients for a well-stocked kitchen, as well as notes on ingredients I mention throughout the book:

**UNBLEACHED ALL-PURPOSE FLOUR:** This is standard white flour, sans the chemicals. You won't notice a difference, I promise.

**EVAPORATED CANE SUGAR:** This is simply regular sugar but unbleached. It is fine like granulated sugar, but it's golden rather than the sickly white color we are more accustomed to seeing. Sometimes it's labeled as "evaporated cane juice" or just "organic sugar."

**MILD VEGETABLE OIL:** This means a basic type of oil, something that has little to no flavor, such as canola, vegetable, or grapeseed oil.

**MILD VINEGAR:** I recommend regular distilled white vinegar or apple cider vinegar. White balsamic can work in a pinch, but I'd recommend against regular balsamic or anything flavored.

**NON-DAIRY MILK OF CHOICE:** Where noted, I have recommended specific types of milks for a reason, but otherwise, I test with a variety of kinds to make sure that the recipes are flexible enough to work with whatever you prefer to use.

**NON-DAIRY MARGARINE:** Look for brands like Earth Balance or Spectrum. Cheap vegetable margarines in the grocery store tend to have trace dairy products in them, in addition to being made with strange hydrogenated oil blends. Plus, most aren't suitable for baking.

**NATURAL PEANUT BUTTER:** Natural peanut butter has a more prominent flavor and is what is called for in this book. If you have peanut butter with added sugar, you may wish to reduce the overall sugar content of a recipe by a couple of teaspoons to ensure your treat is not too sweet.

**SEMISWEET CHOCOLATE CHIPS:** While some semisweet chips have dairy in them, many brands don't and you can find chips labeled as "vegan" at many health food stores.

# VEGAN BAKING: WHAT THE WHAT?

Vegan baking might seem like an insurmountable challenge, but I assure you, it's easy and delicious. You won't miss those eggs or dairy a bit, I promise.

**EGGS:** Eggs provide moisture, leavening, texture, and binding for baked goods. While that sounds like a tall order, replacing them in traditional recipes is much easier than you'd anticipate. When looking to veganize a favorite recipe, look no further than the chart below:

| EGG REPLACER | EQUIVALENT TO 1 EGG | WORKS BEST IN... |
|---|---|---|
| unsweetened applesauce | ¼ cup | quick breads, muffins, cakes, bars, and cookies |
| plain or vanilla non-dairy yogurt | ¼ cup | cakes, bars, quick breads, and muffins |
| "sour" milk | 1 teaspoon mild vinegar plus enough milk to make ¼ cup | cakes, muffins, and quick breads; this works as a hybrid leavener and binder, making things rise and stay moist |
| ground flax seed | 1 tablespoon flax plus 3 tablespoons water, whipped up and then left to set for a few minutes (it gets thick like an egg white) | great for things that are chewy, such as brownies and cookies; also great in yeasted breads, especially sweet ones |
| silken tofu | ¼ cup, puréed | cakes that are slightly dense in texture, pies, quick breads, and muffins |
| assorted puréed/ shredded fruits or veggies | ¼ cup | canned pumpkin, mashed banana, zucchini, carrots, or pears all make great binders, so if they are already in your recipe you can typically omit the eggs and add 1 tablespoon of milk per egg to replace the liquid content |
| Ener-G Egg Replacer | see directions on box | this boxed replacer is not my favorite replacer to use, but is easy to find and shelf stable; it's starch based, so I don't recommend it for things that you want to stay really moist such as cake |

**DAIRY:** Dairy is so easy to work around, it's silly. Long gone are the days of chalky soy milk. Now you can replace milk with loads of alternatives: almond, hemp, rice, hazelnut, sunflower seed, coconut milk, and on and on. There are also great alternatives to butter, including some tasty vegetable oil–based spreads and coconut oil. Several companies make great alternatives for yogurt and thicker creamers.

# CHAPTER 1

# No-Bake Treats

Sometimes you just can't turn on the oven. It's too hot, it's too sticky. Or, sometimes the oven is on the fritz. Either way, the dessert shall go on!

# PEANUT BUTTER CREAM CUPS

These lovely no-bake cups come together quickly with basic ingredients and can be made well in advance. The creamy peanut butter custard gives way to a rich chocolate bottom. They are creamy and decadent without being overly rich—perfect with a cup of coffee or tea.

## INGREDIENTS

¼ cup non-dairy semisweet chocolate chips

1 teaspoon non-dairy margarine or coconut oil (see note)

3 tablespoons non-dairy milk of choice

1 (12.3-ounce) package silken tofu

⅓ cup natural creamy peanut butter

½ to ⅓ cup sifted powdered sugar, to taste

½ teaspoon vanilla extract

non-dairy semisweet chocolate chips and/or salted peanuts, for garnish (optional)

**Makes 6 cream cups**

## DIRECTIONS

🍮 Set out six 4-ounce canning jars. In a small microwave-safe bowl, melt the chocolate chips, margarine or coconut oil, and milk in the microwave in 10 second increments, stirring every 15 seconds, until smooth. Divide the chocolate mixture among the jars, coating the bottoms (about 1 tablespoon per jar).

🍮 In a food processor or blender, combine the tofu and peanut butter, scraping the sides down as needed, until smooth. Add the powdered sugar and vanilla, starting with ½ cup sugar and adding more until you reach your desired sweetness.

🍮 Divide the peanut butter mousse among the jars (about ⅓ cup per jar). If desired, top with additional chocolate chips or peanuts to garnish, then screw on the lids. Refrigerate for at least 30 minutes before serving. These keep in the fridge for up to 4 days.

**NOTE:** If you use the coconut oil, the chocolate will get firmer in the fridge the longer it chills. If you want it to soften, just let the pudding come to room temperature for a few minutes before serving.

# RAW PECAN PIE

Raw pecan pie was one of the first raw desserts I ever had. I was scared of raw food and thought I hated pecan pie, but this instantly became one of my favorite desserts. Raw desserts are very rich, so it doesn't hurt to share...or at least pace yourself.

## INGREDIENTS

**CRUST:**

1 cup chopped raw walnuts

½ cup chopped raw pecans

¾ cup chopped pitted dates

sprinkle of salt

**FILLING:**

1½ cups raw halved cashews

1 cup chopped raw pecans

½ cup chopped pitted dates

2 tablespoons to ¼ cup water

¼ teaspoon ground cinnamon

sprinkle of freshly grated nutmeg

whole raw pecans, for garnish (optional)

**Makes 6 pies**

## DIRECTIONS

To make the crust, combine all the ingredients in a food processor and pulse until the dough comes together in a thick ball, scraping down the sides as needed. Divide the crust mixture among six 4-ounce canning jars and press to cover the bottoms and up the sides to about ½ inch under the rim.

For the filling, briefly soak the cashews, pecans, and pitted dates in water to soften, about 15 minutes. Reserving ¼ cup of the water, drain and place the cashews, pecans, and dates in the bowl of a food processor. Blend, adding the reserved water as needed, 1 tablespoon at a time, until creamy and spreadable. Add the cinnamon and nutmeg, and pulse to combine.

Divide and spread the filling among the prepared jars. Top with whole pecans, if using. Refrigerate for at least 1 hour before serving.

# BANANA CREAM PIE CRUNCH CUPS

These pies are so simple and perfect for a hot day: the "crust" goes on top and is actually a granola that you make on the stovetop and then sprinkle over the creamy banana filling. The granola features crunchy almonds and a kiss of maple, making this treat simply sublime.

## INGREDIENTS

2 large, ripe bananas, divided

2 recipes Creamy Custard (page 107)

### MAPLE GRANOLA CRUNCH:

4 tablespoons non-dairy margarine or coconut oil

3 tablespoons maple syrup

¼ cup packed brown sugar

1 teaspoon vanilla extract

½ teaspoon maple extract

2 cups old-fashioned rolled oats (not quick-cooking)

¼ teaspoon ground cinnamon

¼ cup chopped walnuts

sprinkle of salt

**Makes 6 pie cups**

## DIRECTIONS

Mash one of the bananas. Make the Creamy Custard recipe, mixing in the mashed banana at the end. Refrigerate to chill. Reserve other banana.

To make the maple granola, in a large skillet, melt the margarine or coconut oil over medium heat. Add the maple syrup, brown sugar, vanilla, and maple extract. Incorporate the oats and cinnamon and stir to coat. Stirring often, cook the oat mixture until the liquid is absorbed, the oats begin to toast a little, and the granola turns a golden brown, about 10 minutes. Add the walnuts and sprinkle of salt, and stir to combine.

Remove the granola from the heat and let it cool. Slice the remaining banana into ¼-inch coins.

To assemble the cups, use 6 half-pint canning jars. Fill each jar about ⅓ of the way full with the banana cream, then add a layer of banana slices. Fill the jars with more banana cream to about ¾ inch below the rim. Top each jar with a scoop of the maple granola crunch and garnish with the remaining banana slices.

# ICE CREAM CAKE CUPS

Petite, personal-sized ice cream cakes, à la the classic one we all grew up with, are a hit with kids and adults alike.

## INGREDIENTS

1 recipe Chocolate Ganache (page 109)

1 pint (2 cups) non-dairy chocolate ice cream

6 crushed chocolate sandwich cookies

1 pint (2 cups) non-dairy vanilla ice cream

½ recipe Coconut Whipped Cream (page 111)

**Makes 6 cake cups**

## DIRECTIONS

🍫 Cool the Chocolate Ganache until it's warm but still spreadable. Let the chocolate ice cream sit out at room temperature until easily scoopable. Set out 6 half-pint canning jars. Scoop ⅓ cup of chocolate ice cream into the bottom of each jar, packing it down well with the back of a spoon. Sprinkle one crushed cookie into each jar.

🍫 Spread the ganache among the jars and smooth over top of the cookie crumbles. Refrigerate the jars for about 30 minutes, until the ganache is slightly firmed up. While they are in the fridge, let the vanilla ice cream soften. Once the ganache is firm to the touch (it might still be a little tacky; that's fine), top each jar with ⅓ cup of the vanilla ice cream. Pack it down. You can either spread the Coconut Cream on top of the ice cream, as a frosting, or you can pipe it out with a pastry bag to decorate.

🍫 Freeze the ice cream cups for at least 3 hours before serving.

# RAW-BERRY CREAM PIE

Oh boy, oh boy. Creamy cashews. Mellow, sweet dates. Bright, juicy strawberries. You will be the most popular person at the potluck when you present your friends with these little jars of happiness.

## INGREDIENTS

**CRUST:**

2 cups chopped raw walnuts

¾ cup chopped pitted dates

sprinkle of salt

**FILLING:**

2 cups raw cashews

½ cup chopped pitted dates

2 tablespoons to ¼ cup water

¼ vanilla bean, scraped

2 cups hulled, halved fresh strawberries

**Makes 6 pies**

## DIRECTIONS

To make the crust, combine all the ingredients in a food processor and pulse until the dough comes together in a thick ball, scraping down the sides as needed. Divide the crust mixture among six 4-ounce canning jars and press to cover the bottoms and up the sides of the jars to about ½ inch under the rim.

For the filling, briefly soak the cashews and pitted dates in water to soften, about 15 minutes. Reserving ¼ cup of the water, drain and place the cashews, dates, and scraped vanilla bean seeds in the bowl of a food processor. Blend, adding the reserved water as needed, 1 tablespoon at a time, until creamy and spreadable.

Fill each jar with strawberries, reserving 1 berry half per jar for garnish, if desired. Top with filling and smooth to fill each prepared jar. Garnish with the remaining strawberries, if using.

# CHOCOLATE VANILLA PUDDIN' CUPS

Classic pudding cups are a must-have. Whether you like your pudding warm or cold, these little cups are sure to delight everyone. Soy or hemp milk will help make a richer pudding, but other non-dairy milks work fine in this recipe.

## INGREDIENTS

**VANILLA PUDDING:**

⅓ cup evaporated cane sugar

3 tablespoons cornstarch

2 cups non-dairy milk of choice

1 tablespoon non-dairy margarine

1 teaspoon vanilla extract

**CHOCOLATE PUDDING:**

⅓ cup evaporated cane sugar

2 tablespoons cornstarch

2 tablespoons unsweetened baking cocoa, sifted

2 cups non-dairy milk of choice

¼ cup non-dairy semisweet chocolate chips

1 tablespoon non-dairy margarine

1 teaspoon vanilla extract

**Makes 6 puddin' cups**

## DIRECTIONS

🥄 To make the vanilla pudding, in a large saucepan, combine the sugar and cornstarch, and whisk until there are no large lumps. Whisk in the milk until combined and cook over medium-high heat, whisking constantly, until the mixture begins to bubble, 7 to 10 minutes. Lower the heat and cook until the pudding is thick and coats the back of a spoon, about 5 more minutes. Remove from the heat and mix in the margarine and vanilla, whisking until combined. Let the pudding cool for about 20 minutes, whisking every few minutes to keep a skin from forming.

🥄 To make the chocolate pudding, in a large saucepan, combine the sugar, cornstarch, and cocoa powder, and whisk until there are no large lumps. Whisk in the milk until combined and cook over medium-high heat, whisking constantly, until the mixture begins to bubble, 7 to 10 minutes. Lower the heat and cook until the pudding is thick and coats the back of a spoon, about 5 more minutes. Remove from the heat and mix in the chocolate chips, margarine, and vanilla extract, whisking until combined. Let the pudding cool for about 20 minutes, whisking every few minutes to keep a skin from forming.

🥄 To make the pudding cups, use a large spoon to layer six 4-ounce canning jars with pudding roughly 2 tablespoons at a time, alternating layers of vanilla and chocolate. Gently rock the jars to help the layers settle. If you're anti–pudding skin, you can press waxed paper or plastic wrap against the top layer of pudding in each jar to keep a skin from forming. Pudding can be enjoyed warm, or refrigerate for at least 2 hours if you prefer a cold pudding cup.

# BANANA SPLIT BITES

This take on the classic banana split is the perfect answer to the question "What's for dessert?" when nothing was planned. A well-stocked pantry will have most everything needed for this lazy summer treat.

## INGREDIENTS

1 recipe Chocolate Ganache (page 109)

2 ripe bananas

1 recipe Creamy Custard (page 107)

¼ cup plus 2 tablespoons strawberry jam

2 tablespoons salted halved peanuts (optional)

6 maraschino cherries (optional)

**Makes 6 bites**

## DIRECTIONS

🍌 Set out six 4-ounce canning jars. Divide the ganache in half, and divide one half among the bottoms of each jar.

🍌 Slice the bananas into ¼-inch coins. Divide one of the bananas among the jars. Divide half of the custard among the jars. Repeat one more banana and custard layer. Top with 1 tablespoon of jam on top of each jar and then divide the remaining ganache on top.

🍌 Sprinkle peanuts over top of the ganache and crown it with a cherry, if desired.

# SALTY CRUNCHY ALMOND CHEESECAKE

Salty/sweet is a popular flavor combination these days, and who can blame anyone for seeking it out? This no-bake treat is the perfect combination of crunchy, salty pretzels, a thin layer of chocolate, and creamy, almond-scented cheesecake.

## INGREDIENTS

3 cups crumbled salted pretzels

1 recipe Chocolate Ganache (page 109)

1 (12.3-ounce) package silken tofu

1 (8-ounce) package non-dairy cream cheese

⅔ cup evaporated cane sugar

½ teaspoon cornstarch

½ to 1 teaspoon almond extract

almond slivers or chocolate-covered pretzels, for garnish

**Makes 6 cheesecakes**

## DIRECTIONS

Divide the pretzels among 6 half-pint canning jars. Divide the ganache and drizzle over the top of the pretzel layers. Do your best to make an even layer, as this will create a barrier and help keep the pretzels crunchy. Refrigerate the jars.

In a food processor, place the tofu, cream cheese, sugar, cornstarch, and almond extract and process to combine. Scrape down the sides of the bowl as needed until the mixture is creamy and uniform. Taste and add more almond extract as needed, depending on strength. If you're not serving the cheesecakes the same day, keep in mind that the extract will intensify as they sit.

Divide the almond cream among the jars, cover, and refrigerate for at least 2 hours before serving. Garnish with almonds or chocolate-covered pretzels before serving.

# GRASSHOPPER PIES

Chocolate and mint are such a lovely pairing, and this no-bake treat is a perfect way to indulge. And as I always say, never miss an opportunity to beat on something with your rolling pin.

## INGREDIENTS

12 crushed chocolate sandwich cookies

1 tablespoon plus 1 teaspoon non-dairy margarine, melted

1 (12.3-ounce) container silken tofu

1 (8-ounce) container non-dairy cream cheese

⅔ to ¾ cup evaporated cane sugar

1 teaspoon cornstarch

½ to ¾ teaspoon peppermint extract

green food coloring (optional)

**Makes 6 pies**

## DIRECTIONS

🍃 In a medium bowl, combine the crushed sandwich cookies and the melted margarine, stirring until combined. Divide it evenly among six 4-ounce canning jars. You can either press it into one thick bottom layer or press it down evenly on the bottom and halfway up the sides of the jars. Refrigerate.

🍃 In a food processor, place the tofu, cream cheese, ⅔ cup sugar, cornstarch, and ½ teaspoon peppermint extract, and process to combine. Scrape down the sides of the bowl as needed until the mixture is creamy and uniform. Taste and adjust the sweetness and peppermint as needed (remember that the peppermint flavor will get more intense as it chills). Add a couple of drops of green food coloring, if using, and mix well.

🍃 Remove the cookie crusts from the fridge and evenly spoon the peppermint cream over the top of each crust. Refrigerate for at least 2 hours before serving to allow the cream to set and the flavors to meld.

## ●●● CHAPTER 2

# Cakelettes

If you were to pit these jar-encased cakelettes up against regular old cupcakes in the Octagon, rest assured that these tasty morsels would emerge the victor. Your days are numbered, cupcakes.

# BASIC CHOCOLATE CAKE

This is the little black dress of cakes. It takes a strange duck to turn down moist, tender chocolate cake and rest assured, this cake has never been stood up. Serve it with a healthy schmear of Chocolate Buttercream Frosting or some lovely Berry Sauce or, if you're feeling decadent, a little of both.

## INGREDIENTS

1⅓ cups unbleached all-purpose flour

⅓ cup unsweetened baking cocoa, sifted

⅔ cup evaporated cane sugar

½ teaspoon baking powder

½ teaspoon baking soda

⅛ teaspoon salt

1 cup non-dairy milk of choice

¼ cup non-dairy semisweet chocolate chips

⅓ cup mild vegetable oil

2 teaspoons vanilla extract

Chocolate Buttercream Frosting (page 106) or Berry Sauce (page 113), to serve

**Makes 6 cakes**

## DIRECTIONS

🍫 Preheat the oven to 350°F. Lightly grease six 4-ounce canning jars and place them on a rimmed baking sheet.

🍫 In a small bowl, combine the flour, cocoa, sugar, baking powder, baking soda, and salt. In a large bowl, combine the milk and chocolate chips. Microwave in 15-second increments, stirring after each one, until the chocolate has melted and you can whisk them together. Add the oil and the vanilla to the chocolate mixture and whisk. Add the dry ingredients to the wet in two batches, whisking until just combined.

🍫 Bake for 16 to 19 minutes, until a toothpick inserted into a cake comes out clean. Let the cakes cool on a cooling rack. Wait until completely cool before frosting with buttercream or topping with berry sauce.

# OVER THE RAINBOW CAKES

For a quick snack, these can be baked in a tall half-pint jar, topped with a lovely vanilla buttercream, screwed with a lid, and packed into a lunchbox or bag to nosh at Pride.

There are natural food coloring drops available. Just be aware that the colors are much more subdued than conventional varieties and will yield a lovely pastel rainbow.

## INGREDIENTS

1⅓ cups unbleached all-purpose flour

¾ cup evaporated cane sugar

¾ teaspoon baking powder

¼ teaspoon baking soda

¼ teaspoon salt

1 cup non-dairy milk of choice

⅓ cup mild vegetable oil

½ teaspoon mild vinegar

1 teaspoon vanilla extract

food coloring in several colors

1 recipe Buttercream Frosting (page 106)

**Makes 6 cakes**

## DIRECTIONS

☛ Preheat the oven to 350°F. If you want lots of frosting on the cakes, lightly grease 6 extra-tall half-pint canning jars; if going for more of a cupcake look, use six 4-ounce canning jars. Set the jars on a rimmed baking sheet.

☛ In a bowl, combine the flour, sugar, baking powder, baking soda, and salt. In a large bowl, whisk together the milk, oil, vinegar, and vanilla. Add the dry ingredients to the wet in two batches, whisking until just combined.

☛ Divide the batter among 5 small bowls (about ½ cup per bowl) and add a couple of drops of food coloring to each bowl to make your desired colors. Spoon 1 full tablespoon of each color into each canning jar, layering them one on top of each other. Remember our old friend from art class, ROY G BIV, if you need help remembering which order the colors go in.

☛ Bake for 18 to 22 minutes, until a toothpick comes out clean. If there are moist crumbs, that is fine. Once the cakes are completely cool, pipe the buttercream on top.

# CREAM-FILLED CARROT CAKES

A spin on the traditional carrot cake, these moist, spiced cakes are bursting with cream filling for a truly delicious surprise. You can get creative with how to top them—an additional dollop of filling, some nuts, or try your hand at some fancy carrot flowers.

## INGREDIENTS

1⅓ cups unbleached all-purpose flour

1 teaspoon baking powder

1 teaspoon pumpkin pie spice

1½ teaspoons ground cinnamon

½ teaspoon baking soda

¼ teaspoon salt

½ cup packed brown sugar

¼ cup mild vegetable oil

½ cup unsweetened applesauce

½ cup non-dairy milk of choice

1 teaspoon vanilla extract

1 cup finely shredded carrots

2 tablespoons chopped walnuts

2 tablespoons raisins

1 recipe Cream Cheese Filling (page 111)

**Makes six 4-ounce cakes or 3 half-pint cakes**

## DIRECTIONS

🥄 Preheat the oven to 350°F. Lightly grease six 4-ounce canning jars or 3 half-pint jars.

🥄 In a small bowl, combine the flour, baking powder, pumpkin pie spice, cinnamon, baking soda, and salt. In a larger bowl, cream together the sugar and vegetable oil with an electric mixer. Add the applesauce, milk, and vanilla, and mix until combined. Add the dry ingredients to the wet in two batches, until just mixed. Then add the carrots, walnuts, and raisins, gently mixing to combine.

🥄 Divide the batter among the jars, filling ⅔ of the way full. Bake for 16 to 20 minutes for the 4-ounce jars or 22 to 26 minutes for the half-pints, until a toothpick inserted into a cake comes out clean. Let the cakes cool on a wire rack.

🥄 While the cakes are cooling, prepare the Cream Cheese Filling. Once cooled, fit a pastry bag with a large star or other open tip and fill with the filling. Pushing it down into the center of each cakelette, gently apply pressure, piping the cake full of cream until you see the cake slightly rise from the pressure. You can feel free to pipe in the filling in multiple spots, to ensure you reach maximum cream-filling capacity. Wipe off any oozing custard with a clean paper towel. You can top the cakes in a variety of ways, from adding a dollop of cream filling on top to decorating with additional nuts and raisins.

# ALMOND JOY PUDDING CAKES

Uh, hello. A moist and tender chocolate cake sits atop creamy chocolate pudding, rich with coconut and chunks of almonds. Decadent? Absolutely. Simple? No doubt. You've had a long day, you deserve a luscious treat. Indulge...

## INGREDIENTS

**CAKE:**

¾ cup shredded sweetened coconut

¾ cup chopped almonds

1 cup unbleached all-purpose flour

¼ cup unsweetened baking cocoa, sifted

½ cup evaporated cane sugar

2 teaspoons baking powder

⅛ teaspoon salt

2 tablespoons coconut oil, melted

½ cup non-dairy milk of choice

1 teaspoon almond extract

½ teaspoon vanilla extract

½ cup non-dairy semisweet chocolate chips

**TOPPING:**

⅓ cup evaporated cane sugar

3 tablespoons unsweetened baking cocoa

1 cup boiling water

**Makes 6 cakes**

## DIRECTIONS

To make the cake, preheat the oven to 350°F. Lightly grease 6 half-pint canning jars and place on a rimmed baking sheet. Divide the shredded coconut and almonds among the jars, placing 3 tablespoons of each in the bottom of each jar.

In a small bowl, combine the flour, cocoa, sugar, baking powder, and salt. In a large bowl, whisk together the coconut oil, milk, almond extract, and vanilla extract. In two batches, combine the dry ingredients with the wet until just combined. Fold in the chocolate chips.

For the topping, stir together the sugar and cocoa in a small bowl until well combined

Spread ⅓ cup of batter into the bottom of each jar. Sprinkle 1 heaping tablespoon of the sugar-cocoa mixture on top of each jar, then spoon 3 tablespoons of the boiling water on top of each one. It will look muddy, but trust the process.

Bake for 16 to 20 minutes, until the cake rises to the top and the pudding bubbles around the edges. The cake should seem to float, and a toothpick inserted into a cake should still come out very wet. Let cool 15 minutes on a wire rack before serving.

# BERRY BANANA TRIFLE

This trifle recipe is light and delicious, perfect for picnics or outdoor events. Assemble them, screw on the lids, and toss them in a cooler—you'll be the most popular kid in town when you present your guests with these lovely, light, and refreshing treats. This recipe utilizes a creamy vanilla custard, cubed moist and tender banana cake, and whatever berries you please.

## INGREDIENTS

1½ cups unbleached all-purpose flour

2 teaspoons baking powder

½ teaspoon baking soda

¼ teaspoon salt

⅓ cup neutral-tasting oil

½ cup packed brown sugar

1 cup mashed banana (about 2 bananas)

⅓ cup non-dairy milk of choice

1 recipe Creamy Custard (page 107)

2 cups assorted berries, large ones halved

**Makes 6 trifles**

## DIRECTIONS

🍡 Preheat the oven to 350°F. Lightly grease an 8 x 8-inch square pan.

🍡 In a small bowl, combine the flour, baking powder, baking soda, and salt. In a large bowl, whisk together the oil and sugar until creamy. Add bananas and milk and mix. Add the dry ingredients to the wet ingredients and whisk until just combined.

🍡 Spread into the prepared pan and bake for 32 to 38 minutes, until golden and a toothpick inserted into the center comes out clean. Let cool in the pan on a wire rack for 30 minutes. Run a knife around the edge to loosen the bread, and turn out of the pan to let finish cooling on a rack. Once cooled, cut into ¾-inch cubes.

🍡 While the bread is baking, make the custard and allow it to cool. Using 6 half-pint canning jars, layer the banana cake, custard, and berries, starting with one layer of cake cubes, then custard, then berries, and repeat.

🍡 Refrigerate until ready to serve.

# STRAWBERRY SHORTCAKES

What's better than strawberry shortcake? Strawberries, cake, and coconut cream, nestled together in a portable jar, that's what.

## INGREDIENTS

1⅓ cups unbleached all-purpose flour

⅔ cup plus 2 tablespoons evaporated cane sugar, divided

½ teaspoon baking powder

½ teaspoon baking soda

⅛ teaspoon salt

1 cup non-dairy milk of choice

½ teaspoon mild vinegar

⅓ cup mild vegetable oil

2 teaspoons vanilla extract

3 cups chopped fresh strawberries

1 recipe Coconut Whipped Cream (page 111)

**Makes 6 cakes**

## DIRECTIONS

🍂 Preheat the oven to 350°F. Lightly grease 6 tall, skinny half-pint canning jars and place them on a rimmed baking sheet.

🍂 In a small bowl, combine the flour, ⅔ cup of the sugar, and the baking powder, baking soda, and salt. In a large bowl, whisk together the milk and vinegar. Add the oil and the vanilla and whisk. Add the dry ingredients to the wet in two batches, whisking until just combined.

🍂 Fill each jar ¼ of the way full with batter. Bake for 17 to 20 minutes, or until golden and a toothpick inserted into a jar comes out clean. While the cakes are baking, combine the chopped strawberries and remaining 2 tablespoons of sugar in a large bowl. Cover and refrigerate. Prepare the Coconut Whipped Cream and refrigerate.

🍂 Let the cakes cool on a wire rack. Just before serving, carefully run a butter knife around the edge of each cake and carefully pull it out of the jar. Cut in half, horizontally. Place the bottom piece of the cake back in the jar. Spoon in 2 tablespoons of strawberries and a large dollop of the whipped cream. Top with the second half of the cake and add another layer of berries and cream. Refrigerate until ready to serve.

# BOSTON CREAM CAKES

These simple little cakes are subdued and elegant. A thick, rich ganache gives way to moist yellow cake and a luscious cream filling. Big kids and little kids alike will clamor for more.

## INGREDIENTS

1⅓ cups unbleached all-purpose flour

¾ cup evaporated cane sugar

¾ teaspoon baking powder

¼ teaspoon baking soda

¼ teaspoon salt

1 cup non-dairy milk of choice

⅓ cup mild vegetable oil

½ teaspoon mild vinegar

1 teaspoon vanilla extract

1 recipe Creamy Custard (page 107)

1 recipe Chocolate Ganache (page 109)

**Makes 6 cakes**

## DIRECTIONS

🍮 Preheat the oven to 350°F. Lightly grease six 4-ounce canning jars.

🍮 In a bowl, combine the flour, sugar, baking powder, baking soda, and salt. In a large bowl, whisk together the milk, oil, vinegar, and vanilla. Add the dry ingredients to the wet in two batches, whisking until just combined.

🍮 Place the jars on a rimmed baking sheet and bake for 16 to 20 minutes, until a toothpick inserted into a cake comes out clean. If there are moist crumbs, that is fine. Let the cakes cool completely on a wire rack.

🍮 While the cakes are baking, prepare the Creamy Custard and let it cool. Once the cakes and custard are cooled, prepare the Chocolate Ganache.

🍮 Fit a pastry bag with a large star or other open tip with the Creamy Custard. Pushing it down into the center of each cakelette, gently apply pressure, piping the cake full of cream until you see the cake slightly rise from the pressure. You can feel free to pipe in the filling in multiple spots to ensure you reach maximum cream-filling capacity. Wipe off any oozing custard with a clean paper towel.

🍮 Gently spread ganache over the filled cupcakes. Serve immediately or store covered, in the fridge. Let the cakes sit at room temperature for 15 minutes before serving.

# SPOTTED DICK

The British classic "pudding" is the original cake in a jar. Traditionally it's steamed, but this baked treatment yields a tender cake that's not too shabby for a Yank (and a vegan one, at that!).

## INGREDIENTS

1½ cups unbleached all-purpose flour

½ cup evaporated cane sugar

½ teaspoon baking powder

⅛ teaspoon salt

½ cup non-dairy milk of choice, warmed

¼ cup brown rice syrup or dark agave nectar

3 tablespoons mild vegetable oil

1 teaspoon vanilla extract

½ cup raisins

1 recipe Custard Sauce (page 106)

**Makes 4 or 8 cakes**

## DIRECTIONS

🍠 Preheat the oven 350°F. Lightly grease eight 4-ounce canning jars or 6 half-pint jars and place on a rimmed baking sheet.

🍠 In a small bowl, combine the flour, sugar, baking powder, and salt. In a large bowl, whisk together the milk, brown rice syrup or agave, oil, and vanilla. Incorporate the dry ingredients in batches, until just combined. Gently incorporate the raisins.

🍠 Fill each jar ⅔ of the way with the batter. Bake for 17 to 20 minutes for small jars or 23 to 27 minutes for large jars. Let the jars cool on a wire rack for at least 20 minutes before serving.

🍠 To serve, run a knife around the edge of the cake to loosen it. Invert onto a plate and top with Custard Sauce.

# MARBLE CAKES WITH HOT FUDGE

Chocolate and vanilla lovers of the world unite! This cake is moist and flavorful, and the swirl is so pretty. Topped with a little hot fudge, it's simply out of this world.

## INGREDIENTS

1⅓ cups unbleached all-purpose flour

⅔ cup plus 1 tablespoon evaporated cane sugar, divided

½ teaspoon baking powder

½ teaspoon baking soda

¼ teaspoon salt

1¼ cups non-dairy milk of choice, divided

½ teaspoon mild vinegar

⅓ cup mild vegetable oil

2 teaspoons vanilla extract

3 tablespoons unsweetened baking cocoa, sifted

2 tablespoons grated or shaved chocolate

1 recipe Hot Fudge Sauce (page 110)

**Makes 6 cakes**

## DIRECTIONS

🍫 Preheat the oven to 350°F. Lightly grease six 4-ounce canning jars and place on a rimmed baking sheet.

🍫 In a small bowl, combine the flour, ⅔ cup of the sugar, and the baking powder, baking soda, and salt. In a large bowl, combine 1 cup of the milk and the vinegar. Whisk in the vegetable oil and vanilla. In a third bowl, combine the cocoa with the remaining 1 tablespoon sugar. Whisk to break up any clumps. Add the remaining ¼ cup milk and the grated or shaved chocolate and stir to create a chocolaty paste.

🍫 Combine the flour mixture with the milk and vinegar mixture in two batches, mixing until just combined. Roughly divide the batter, mixing half into the bowl with the chocolate paste. Stir until just incorporated.

🍫 Spoon alternating tablespoons of vanilla and chocolate batter into the prepared jars, filling ⅔ of the way full. Draw a butter knife through the batter several times to swirl the flavors together.

🍫 Bake for 16 to 19 minutes, until a toothpick comes out clean. Let the cakes cool on a cooling rack for at least 20 minutes before serving with Hot Fudge Sauce.

# LEMON PUDDING CAKES

This is a recipe that can cause you to think, "Uh, oh." Before it goes into the oven, its fate appears dubious, but the oven gods work their magic. The moist cake floats to the top while the tangy pudding sinks to the bottom—kitchen chemistry at its finest. For saucier cakes, reduce the cooking time by 2 minutes.

## INGREDIENTS

**PUDDING:**

¼ cup evaporated cane sugar

1 teaspoon grated lemon zest

¼ cup fresh lemon juice (from 1 large lemon or 2 small lemons)

¾ cup hot water

**CAKE:**

1 cup unbleached all-purpose flour

⅓ cup evaporated cane sugar

1 teaspoon baking powder

½ cup non-dairy milk of choice

2 tablespoons mild vegetable oil

1 teaspoon grated lemon zest

½ teaspoon vanilla extract

**Makes 6 cakes**

## DIRECTIONS

🖛 Preheat the oven to 350°F. Lightly grease six 4-ounce canning jars and place on a large rimmed baking sheet.

🖛 Begin by prepping the pudding ingredients. In a small bowl, mix together the sugar and lemon zest. Set aside. In a small stockpot, combine the lemon juice and water and bring to a boil. Once boiling, turn off the heat, but leave the pot on the burner.

🖛 To make the cake, combine the flour, cane sugar, and baking powder in a small bowl. In a larger bowl, whisk together the milk, vegetable oil, lemon zest, and vanilla to combine. Add the dry ingredients to the wet in two batches and mix until just combined.

🖛 Fill each of the jars halfway with the cake batter. Top the batter with 1½ teaspoons of the sugar-zest mixture. Pour 3 tablespoons of the water–lemon juice mixture on top of each jar. DO NOT COMBINE. It will look scary, but trust me.

🖛 Bake the cakes for 14 to 16 minutes, until the cake has risen and is golden and the lemon pudding is bubbling underneath and around the edges. Let the cakes cool on a wire rack for at least 15 minutes before serving.

# RUSTIC RHUBARB CAKES

Studded within these little cakes, rhubarb shines all on its own. Simple and elegant, without being too sweet, the crunch of sugar on top gives way to tender cake with tart rhubarb goodness.

## INGREDIENTS

1¼ cups unbleached all-purpose flour

½ cup quick-cooking oats

⅔ cup evaporated cane sugar

½ teaspoon baking powder

¼ teaspoon ground cinnamon

⅛ teaspoon salt

1 cup non-dairy milk of choice

½ teaspoon mild vinegar

¼ cup mild vegetable oil

1 teaspoon vanilla extract

1 cup chopped rhubarb, in ½-inch chunks

coarse sugar, for sprinkling

**Makes 4 or 8 cakes**

## DIRECTIONS

Preheat the oven to 350°F. Lightly grease eight 4-ounce canning jars or 4 half-pint canning jars. Place the jars on a rimmed baking sheet.

In a small bowl, combine the flour, oats, sugar, baking powder, cinnamon, and salt. In a large bowl, whisk the milk, vinegar, oil, and vanilla to combine. Add the dry ingredients to the wet in two batches, mixing until just combined. Gently fold in the rhubarb.

Fill each jar ⅔ of the way full with batter. Sprinkle the tops of each cake with a little of the coarse sugar.

Bake for 23 to 26 minutes for large jars and 16 to 20 for smaller jars, until they are golden and a toothpick inserted into a cake comes out clean.

# TIRAMISU

Tender cake, moist with coffee and topped with a creamy counterpart is the best way to end a meal. These cakes need to be prepared ahead of time and chilled, so it's the perfect recipe to put together early in the day so your post-dinner prep is minimal.

## INGREDIENTS

1⅓ cups unbleached all-purpose flour

¾ cup evaporated cane sugar

¾ teaspoon baking powder

¼ teaspoon baking soda

¼ teaspoon salt

1 cup non-dairy milk of choice

⅓ cup mild vegetable oil

½ teaspoon mild vinegar

1 teaspoon vanilla extract

1 recipe Creamy Custard (page 107)

¼ cup strong brewed coffee

2 tablespoons unsweetened baking cocoa powder, sifted

**Makes 6 cakes**

## DIRECTIONS

🍮 Preheat the oven to 350°F. Lightly grease six 4-ounce canning jars. Place the jars on a rimmed baking sheet.

🍮 In a bowl, combine the flour, sugar, baking powder, baking soda, and salt. In a large bowl, whisk together the milk, oil, vinegar, and vanilla. Add the dry ingredients to the wet in two batches, mixing until just combined. Fill each jar halfway with batter.

🍮 Bake for 16 to 20 minutes, until a toothpick inserted into a cake comes out clean. If there are moist crumbs, that is fine. Let the cakes cool on a wire rack most of the way.

🍮 While the cakes are baking, prepare the Creamy Custard and let it cool. Prepare the coffee and set aside.

🍮 Pour 2 teaspoons of the coffee over each cake, distributing as evenly as possible. Whisk up the Creamy Custard to blend any lumps. Divide the cream over the top of each cake, smoothing the tops. Cover and refrigerate for at least 2 hours before serving.

🍮 Right before serving, dust each jar with 1 teaspoon of cocoa powder on top.

# ELVIS IN A JAR

The peanut butter–banana combo needs no explanation. It's no wonder that it was a favorite of the King's. Add some chocolate and now we're really talking.

## INGREDIENTS

1½ cups unbleached all-purpose flour

2 teaspoons baking powder

½ teaspoon baking soda

¼ teaspoon salt

⅓ cup mild vegetable oil

½ cup packed brown sugar

1 cup mashed banana (about 2 bananas)

⅓ cup non-dairy milk of choice

1 teaspoon vanilla extract

1 recipe Peanut Butter Filling (page 7)

1 recipe Chocolate Ganache (page 109)

salted whole or halved peanuts, for garnish (optional)

**Makes 6 cakes**

## DIRECTIONS

🍗 Preheat oven to 350°F. Lightly grease and flour six 4-ounce canning jars. Place on a rimmed baking sheet and set aside.

🍗 In a small bowl, combine the flour, baking powder, baking soda, and salt. In a larger bowl, whisk the oil and sugar until creamy. Add the banana, milk, and vanilla, and whisk well. Add the dry ingredients to the wet in two batches, whisking until just mixed.

🍗 Divide the batter evenly among the jars, filling just over halfway. Bake for 14 to 17 minutes, until a toothpick inserted into a cake comes out clean. Let cool completely on a rack.

🍗 While the cakes are baking, make the Peanut Butter Filling and let cool in the fridge.

🍗 Just before assembling, make the Chocolate Ganache and set aside. Fill a pastry bag fitted with a large star tip with the Peanut Butter Filling. Insert the tip into the top of each banana cake, gently piping until you see the cake gently rise and resist. Remove the tip and repeat with each cake.

🍗 If you have extra filling, I sometimes like to spread a healthy schmear on top of each cake and smooth it out. Then divide the ganache among the jars and gently smooth over top of the peanut butter–filled cakes. Garnish with peanuts, if desired.

# APRICOT ALMOND CAKE

Fragrant apricot jam soaks into the bottom of a tender almond cake, creating an elegant grown-up treat; it's so tasty that you will feel good about hiding in the kitchen to chow down on a second helping.

## INGREDIENTS

1 cup apricot jam

1½ cups unbleached all-purpose flour

⅓ cup almond meal

⅔ cup evaporated cane sugar

½ teaspoon baking powder

¼ teaspoon ground cinnamon

⅛ teaspoon salt

1 cup non-dairy milk of choice

½ teaspoon mild vinegar

3 tablespoons mild vegetable oil

1 teaspoon vanilla extract

½ cup chopped almonds

**Makes 4 or 8 cakes**

## DIRECTIONS

Preheat the oven to 350°F. Lightly grease eight 4-ounce canning jars or 4 half-pint canning jars. Place the jars on a rimmed baking sheet and divide the apricot jam between the prepared jars.

In a small bowl, combine the flour, almond meal, sugar, baking powder, cinnamon, and salt. In a large bowl, whisk together the milk, vinegar, oil, and vanilla. Add the dry ingredients to the wet in two batches, whisking until just combined.

Fill each jar ⅔ of the way full. Gently smooth the batter and top with a sprinkle of the chopped almonds.

Bake for 23 to 26 minutes for large jars and 16 to 20 minutes for smaller jars, until the cakes are golden and a toothpick inserted in the center of a cake comes out clean of batter (there might be some apricot jam; that's fine).

Let cool on a wire rack for 20 minutes before serving.

# S'MORES IN A JAR

These s'mores are a riff on the classic: graham cracker–flavored cake covered in a layer of creamy chocolate ganache and then topped with vegan marshmallows, lightly broiled to brown them. There are several companies that make vegan marshmallows, and you should be able to find them at your local health food store or online.

## INGREDIENTS

1⅓ cups unbleached all-purpose flour

⅔ cup evaporated cane sugar

1½ teaspoons ground cinnamon

¾ teaspoon baking powder

¼ teaspoon baking soda

¼ teaspoon salt

1 cup non-dairy milk of choice

¼ cup mild vegetable oil

2 tablespoons maple syrup or agave nectar

1 tablespoon molasses

1 teaspoon vanilla extract

1 recipe Chocolate Ganache (page 109)

1 cup vegan marshmallows (see note)

**Makes 6 cakes**

## DIRECTIONS

🍫 Preheat the oven to 350°F. Lightly grease 6 half-pint canning jars. Wide-mouth jars work best for these. Set the jars on a rimmed baking sheet.

🍫 In a bowl, combine the flour, sugar, cinnamon, baking powder, baking soda, and salt. In a large bowl, whisk together the milk, oil, maple syrup or agave, molasses, and vanilla. Add the dry ingredients to the wet in two batches, whisking until just combined.

🍫 Fill each prepared jar ½ full of batter and bake for 18 to 22 minutes, until a toothpick inserted into a cake comes out clean. If there are moist crumbs, that is fine. Let the cakes cool on a cooling rack. While the cakes are cooling, prepare the Chocolate Ganache.

🍫 Spread ganache over tops of the cooled cakes (it's fine if they are still warm). At this point, you can reserve the cakes for serving later or proceed. These cakes are best served warm and gooey, but you can always reheat them from room temp by either toasting them in the oven at 350°F for 2 to 3 minutes or microwaving for 45 seconds to 1 minute. If you microwave them, remember to remove the lid and ring!

🍫 Right before serving, preheat the oven's broiler to high. Divide the marshmallows and sprinkle them on top of each jar. Place the jars under the broiler, with at least 1 inch of space, for 30 seconds to 1 minute, until the marshmallows are lightly browned.

**NOTE:** The two leading vegan marshmallow companies make fairly large marshmallows. If you would like smaller pieces to top your jars, cut the marshmallows with a sharp knife, then dust the exposed edges with powdered sugar to keep them from sticking.

# CHAPTER 3

# Pie and Friends

Pie isn't just a food: it's a lifestyle. You have your pie days, sure, but other days are better suited for a crisp or a cobbler. And then there are those crumble occasions. Never fear, you're covered.

# FLAKY PASTRY CRUST

This pastry crust is all you could ever ask for—tender and moist, it browns nicely and results in a flaky crust that will make your granny jealous. If you use a food processor to pull it together, you'll be the big winner because then it's completely effortless.

## INGREDIENTS

1¼ cups unbleached all-purpose flour

1 teaspoon evaporated cane sugar

⅛ teaspoon salt

8 tablespoons (1 stick) cold non-dairy margarine, cut into chunks

1 to 2 tablespoons cold water

**Makes 6 to 8 mini pie crusts**

## DIRECTIONS

In a bowl or food processor, combine the flour, sugar, and salt. Using a pastry blender or strong fork, work in the cold margarine until it resembles a coarse meal; if using the processor, add the margarine and pulse to form a coarse meal. Add just enough water to make the dough come together. Flatten it into a disk, wrap it in plastic wrap or waxed paper, and then refrigerate for at least 30 minutes, or up to 3 days.

# STRAWBERRY RHUBARB PIES

Strawberry and rhubarb are such a heavenly pairing—tangy and sweet, they create a perfect filling underneath a flaky, buttery crust.

## INGREDIENTS

1 pound rhubarb, cut into ½-inch cubes

1 pound fresh strawberries, hulled and cut into ½-inch cubes

¾ cup evaporated cane sugar

3 tablespoons cornstarch

2 recipes Flaky Pastry Crust (page 43)

non-dairy ice cream, to serve

**Makes 6 pies**

## DIRECTIONS

🍠 In a large bowl, combine the rhubarb and strawberries. In a small bowl, whisk together the sugar and cornstarch. Sprinkle the sugar mixture over the fruit and toss to coat. Let sit for 30 minutes, mixing occasionally.

🍠 Preheat the oven to 350°F. Set out six 4-ounce canning jars on a rimmed baking sheet. Remove the Flaky Pastry Crust from the fridge and divide a little unevenly, about a ⅓ and ⅔ split. Return the smaller piece to the fridge. Divide the large piece into 6 balls. On a floured surface, roll out each ball to about 6 inches in diameter. Place one crust inside each of the jars and flatten across the bottom and up the sides, until it reaches the top and comes over the edge just a little bit. Refrigerate the jars for about 10 minutes.

🍠 Take out the remaining crust and divide into 6 even pieces and roll out on a floured surface, making pie crust tops about 4 inches in diameter, or about 1 inch wider than the tops of your jars. Cut a little vent hole in the middle with a knife or a small cookie cutter.

🍠 Remove the jars from the fridge and divide the strawberry-rhubarb mixture among the jars, filling them rather full, as the filling will shrink once baked. Top each jar with one of the pie tops and pinch the dough to seal with the bottom crust. You might need a little water to get the crust to stick.

🍠 Bake for 23 to 28 minutes, until the crusts are golden and the filling is bubbling from the vent.

🍠 Let the pies cool on a rack for at least 1 hour before serving. The filling needs to set or it will be rather soupy when you dig into it.

🍠 Serve à la mode with your favorite non-dairy ice cream.

# CHERRY CRUMBLE PIE

These sweet little pies are flexible: top them with the crumble or opt to use the pie crust scraps to make darling little lattice tops. Either way, they will be adorable and delicious. You aren't limited to cherries, of course—this recipe will be tasty with berries as well.

## INGREDIENTS

**PIES:**

¼ cup evaporated cane sugar

1½ teaspoons cornstarch

2 cups pitted cherries (fresh or frozen), coarsely chopped

2 tablespoons water

1 teaspoon lemon juice

1 recipe Flaky Pastry Crust (page 43)

**CRUMBLE TOPPING:**

2 tablespoons unbleached all-purpose flour

1 tablespoon oats (quick-cooking or old-fashioned)

1 tablespoon evaporated cane sugar

1 tablespoon cold non-dairy margarine

**Makes 6 pies**

## DIRECTIONS

- Set aside six 4-ounce canning jars.

- Starting with the pie filling, combine the sugar and cornstarch in the bottom of a medium saucepan. Over medium heat, whisk until combined. Add the cherries and water and cook, stirring often, until the sugar mixture is dissolved and the filling starts to thicken and coats the back of a spoon. Remove from the heat and stir in the lemon juice. Let the filling cool.

- Meanwhile, make the crumble topping by combining the flour, oats, and sugar in a bowl. Mix in the margarine by hand, moving quickly to keep from melting the margarine, until it makes a coarse meal. Refrigerate until ready to use.

- Preheat the oven to 350°F. Remove the crust from the fridge and divide into 6 equally sized pieces. Gently roll out the disks on a floured surface until they are 5 to 6 inches across. Press the dough into each jar, creating a ¼-inch-thick crust that covers the bottoms and comes all the way up the sides of the jar. Be sure to work quickly so you don't get the dough too warm. If that happens, just finish putting the crust in the jars and then chill them for 15 minutes before proceeding. If you have remaining crust, you can roll it out and cut it into ⅛-inch strips to create lattice tops for some of the pies. Otherwise, discard any leftover crust.

- Place the jars on a rimmed baking sheet and fill each crust just to the top with pie filling and either top with the crumble or with pie crust. Bake for 23 to 28 minutes, until the topping is golden. Let the pies cool on a wire rack for 30 minutes before serving.

# LEMON MERINGUE PIE

Who doesn't love tangy lemon meringue pie? It's a summer barbecue classic!

## INGREDIENTS

1 recipe Flaky Pastry Crust (page 43)

⅔ cup evaporated cane sugar

2 teaspoons unbleached all-purpose flour

2 teaspoons cornstarch

pinch of salt

¾ cup water

1 teaspoon grated lemon zest

⅓ cup fresh lemon juice

1 recipe Meringue Topping (page 116)

**Makes 6 pies**

## DIRECTIONS

Preheat the oven to 350°F. Place six 4-ounce canning jars on a rimmed baking sheet. Divide the pie crust among the jars and press down firmly into the bottom of each jar, creating a thick, solid layer of crust. Poke with a fork to create some air holes.

Bake for 9 to 12 minutes, until golden and puffy. Remove from oven and let cool on a wire rack.

While the crusts are cooling, prepare the filling. In a medium saucepan, combine the sugar, flour, cornstarch, and salt. Whisk in the water. Bring to a boil over medium heat, stirring constantly. Reduce the heat to low and whisk until thickened, approximately 5 minutes. Add the lemon zest and juice, and whisk to combine. Continue whisking until bubbling in the center, then continue to bubble for 2 to 3 minutes. Remove from the heat and pour into a heatproof bowl. Let sit, stirring occasionally, until fairly cool.

Pour the lemon filling into each jar, filling to ½ inch from the top. Refrigerate for at least 3 hours (preferably overnight) before serving.

Top with each pie with a dollop of the Meringue Topping. If you would like, place the pies under the broiler on low heat, keeping an eye and not exceeding 30 seconds so your meringue doesn't melt. Serve immediately.

# PEACH MELBA COBBLER

Peach melba is a superb flavor combination. Sweet, juicy peaches and tart raspberries work together like best friends to actually taste like summer. Add tender cobbler topping and it's just plain heavenly.

## INGREDIENTS

4 to 5 large peaches, cored and chopped into ½-inch pieces (about 4 cups)

2 cups fresh raspberries

½ cup evaporated cane sugar, divided

1 cup unbleached all-purpose flour

2 teaspoons baking powder

¼ teaspoon salt

2 tablespoons non-dairy margarine, melted

¾ cup non-dairy milk of choice

**Makes 6 cobblers**

## DIRECTIONS

🍐 Preheat the oven to 375°F. Lightly grease 6 half-pint jars. Place the jars on a rimmed baking sheet.

🍐 In a large bowl, combine the peach slices, raspberries, and ¼ cup of the sugar. In a small bowl, combine the flour, baking powder, and salt. Add the margarine and milk and gently mix until just combined.

🍐 Divide the peach mixture between the 6 jars. Top each jar with about ⅓ cup of cobbler topping, filling each to about ½ inch under the rim.

🍐 Bake for 20 to 25 minutes, until the cobbler has risen and is golden and the peaches and raspberries are bubbling. A knife inserted in each jar should yield tender peaches, the cobbler topping should be tender, and the knife should come out clean of batter (there might be fruit juices, though).

🍐 Let the cobblers cool on a wire rack for 15 minutes before serving.

# APPLE CRISP CUPS

Apple crisp is a classic treat and most of the ingredients are usually around your house, so it's quick to throw together when your sweet tooth announces itself. For a twist on the classic, swap out pears for the apples and ground ginger for the cinnamon.

## INGREDIENTS

4 to 5 large, sweet apples, peeled, cored, and sliced into ½-inch pieces (about 5 cups)

⅓ cup plus ¼ cup evaporated cane sugar, divided

1 teaspoon ground cinnamon

1 teaspoon lemon juice

½ cup plus 1 tablespoon unbleached all-purpose flour

½ cup oats (quick-cooking or old-fashioned)

4 tablespoons (¼ cup) cold non-dairy margarine

**Makes 6 crisps**

## DIRECTIONS

Preheat the oven to 350°F. Lightly grease 6 half-pint jars.

In a large bowl, combine the apple slices, ¼ cup of the sugar, and the cinnamon and lemon juice. Toss to combine.

In a small bowl, combine the flour, remaining ⅓ cup sugar, and oats. Using a pastry cutter or the back of a fork, work in the margarine until it becomes a coarse meal.

Fill each jar with apple slices. Pack them well, as the apples will shrink during baking. Pack the top of each jar with the oat mixture. Bake for 25 to 30 minutes, until the topping is golden and the apples are tender when pierced with a knife.

Let the crisps cool on a cooling rack for 20 minutes before serving. If not serving immediately, cover and store in the fridge, and warm them up right before serving.

# WHOLE PLUM PIE

This is one of those recipes that reminds you that all that matters in life is good ingredients. You don't need to get overly fancy to make something that will absolutely rock your taste buds.

## INGREDIENTS

6 small, ripe plums

2 tablespoons evaporated cane sugar

2 recipes Flaky Pastry Crust (page 43)

**Makes 6 pies**

## DIRECTIONS

● Preheat the oven to 375°F. Place six 4-ounce canning jars on a rimmed baking sheet.

● Score each plum into quarters, just to pull out the pit. Sprinkle the cut sides of each plum with 1 teaspoon of sugar.

● Divide the pastry dough into 6 roughly equal balls. On a floured surface, roll out each ball until it's 5 to 6 inches across. Take a plum and place it in the center of a ball of dough, keeping it together so it looks like a whole plum. Wrap the pastry dough up and around the plum, gathering the dough at the top. Leave a little air vent in the pastry, and then place the dough-covered plum into a jar. Repeat with the remaining plums. If you have any scraps or extra bits of dough, you can get creative and add some shapes or cutouts to the exposed parts of the pies.

● Bake the pies for 20 to 25 minutes, until the crust is golden and the plum juices are starting to bubble out of the air hole. Allow the pies to cool on a wire rack for 1 hour before serving.

# KEY LIME PIE

Creamy, luscious key lime pie is nothing short of heavenly. You can use regular limes, but if key limes are available, they are always worth it.

## INGREDIENTS

1 cup raw cashews

1 recipe Flaky Pastry Crust (page 43)

⅔ cup evaporated cane sugar

2 teaspoons unbleached all-purpose flour

2 teaspoons cornstarch

pinch of salt

¾ cup water

1 teaspoon grated lime zest

⅓ cup key lime juice

Coconut Whipped Cream (page 111), to serve

**Makes 6 pies**

## DIRECTIONS

☛ Soak the cashews in a bowl with enough water to cover for 1 hour.

☛ Preheat the oven to 350°F. Place six 4-ounce canning jars on a rimmed baking sheet. Divide the pie crust among the jars and press down firmly into the bottom of each jar, creating a thick, solid layer of crust. Poke with a fork to create some air holes.

☛ Bake for 9 to 12 minutes, until golden and puffy. Remove from the oven and let cool.

☛ While the crusts are cooling, prepare the filling. In a medium saucepan, combine the sugar, flour, cornstarch, and salt. Whisk in the water. Bring to a boil over medium heat, stirring constantly. Reduce the heat to low and whisk until thickened, approximately 5 minutes. Remove from the heat and pour into the bowl of a blender or food processor. Drain the cashews well and add to the bowl. Mix until the nuts are processed and the filling is creamy, stopping to scrape down the sides as needed. Return to the saucepan over medium-low heat, add the lime zest and juice, and whisk to combine. Continue whisking until bubbling in the center, another 3 to 5 minutes. Remove from the heat and transfer to a heatproof bowl. Let sit, stirring occasionally, until fairly cooled.

☛ Pour the lime filling into each jar, filling to ½ inch from the top. Refrigerate the pies for at least 3 hours (preferably overnight), before serving. Top with a dollop of Coconut Whipped Cream just before serving.

# CHOCOLATE BLUEBERRY CRUMBLE

No one ever turns their nose up at blueberry crumble, but add a little chocolate and a hint of balsamic tang and you've turned Grandma's staple into haute cuisine. It's incredible warm, with a little scoop of vanilla ice cream on top, but the leftovers also hold their own. I've never been a fan of cold pizza for breakfast, but a chilled jar of this crumble with coffee is simply sublime.

## INGREDIENTS

**CRUMBLE TOPPING:**

½ cup unbleached all-purpose flour

¼ cup quick-cooking oats

¼ cup evaporated cane sugar

4 tablespoons (¼ cup) cold non-dairy margarine

**FILLING:**

¼ cup evaporated cane sugar

1 tablespoon unsweetened baking cocoa, sifted

2 tablespoons shaved chocolate

1 pint (2 cups) fresh blueberries

1 tablespoon balsamic vinegar

½ teaspoon vanilla extract

**Makes 6 crumbles**

## DIRECTIONS

🍃 For the crumble topping, combine the flour, oats, and sugar in a small bowl. Stir to combine, then cut in the cold margarine using a pastry blender or the back of a strong fork. Blend until it comes together as loose crumbs. Refrigerate until ready to use.

🍃 Preheat the oven to 350°F. Lightly grease six 4-ounce canning jars. Place the jars on a rimmed baking sheet.

🍃 To make the filling, stir together the sugar, cocoa, and shaved chocolate in a large bowl to combine. Toss the blueberries in the mixture. Whisk together the balsamic and vanilla, and sprinkle it over the blueberry mixture. Gently toss to combine.

🍃 Divide the blueberry mixture among the jars. There will be some of the dry mixture that sinks to the bottom of your mixing bowl; sprinkle it over the tops of the berries. Retrieve the crumble topping from the fridge and sprinkle over the top of each jar evenly, gently pressing it down.

🍃 Bake for 15 to 20 minutes, until the topping is golden and the blueberry mixture is bubbling around the edges. Let cool on a rack for 10 minutes before serving.

# CHAPTER 4

# Pastry

Here we find treats more understated in sweetness but bursting with just as much flavor. These bites work equally well in bookending a good meal as they do paired with your morning cup of joe.

# LEMON BLUEBERRY SCONE DOMES

These lovely little scones have a bright citrus taste and a mild sweetness that's perfect paired with a cup of tea. I recommend using Meyer lemons for optimal flavor. Since lemons and blueberries are very summery, in the winter try mixing it up by replacing the lemon with orange and the blueberries with chocolate chips.

## INGREDIENTS

¾ cup unbleached all-purpose flour

½ cup rolled oats (old-fashioned or quick-cooking)

3 tablespoons evaporated cane sugar

1 teaspoon baking powder

1 teaspoon baking soda

¼ teaspoon salt

3 tablespoons cold non-dairy margarine

grated zest and juice of 1 lemon (preferably Meyer)

⅓ cup non-dairy milk of choice

½ cup fresh blueberries

**Makes 6 scones**

## DIRECTIONS

Preheat the oven to 350°F and lightly grease six 4-ounce canning jars. Place the jars on a rimmed baking sheet.

In a medium bowl, combine the flour, oats, sugar, baking powder, baking soda, and salt. Using a pastry blender or the back of a fork, blend in the cold margarine until it resembles a coarse meal. In a small bowl, combine the lemon zest, lemon juice, and milk, then add the liquid to the dry meal and mix until just combined. Add the blueberries and gently combine.

Fill each canning jar to just under the rim. Bake for 17 to 23 minutes or until the scones are risen and golden. Let cool on a rack for 15 minutes before serving.

# CHOCOLATE BABKA BLOSSOMS

These tender little babkas are both tasty and eye-catching, making for a perfect snack with tea or as a sweet brunch treat. This recipe makes 6 large babkas or 12 small, ensuring that no one has to go without. Soy or hemp milks are best here.

## INGREDIENTS

### DOUGH:

⅔ cup warm non-dairy milk of choice

1 (¼-ounce) packet active dry yeast

¼ cup evaporated cane sugar, divided

4 tablespoons (¼ cup) non-dairy margarine, melted

⅛ teaspoon salt

2 cups unbleached all-purpose flour, plus additional for dusting

### FILLING:

3 tablespoons evaporated cane sugar

3 tablespoons unsweetened baking cocoa, sifted

¾ cup chopped non-dairy semisweet chocolate

3 tablespoons non-dairy margarine, melted

¼ cup chopped almonds

**Makes 6 or 12 babkas**

## DIRECTIONS

🍀 To make the cake, place the milk, yeast, and 2 tablespoons of the sugar in a large bowl and let the yeast proof (become foamy) for about 5 minutes. Add the remaining sugar and melted margarine, and whisk. In a medium bowl, mix the salt with the flour and begin to incorporate into the milk mixture, ½ cup at a time, until a soft dough comes together. Gently knead the dough on a floured surface until it is smooth and elastic, 5 to 7 minutes. Place it back in the bowl, cover with a dish towel, and let it rise until doubled in size, about 1½ hours.

🍀 Around the time the dough has risen, make the filling. Mix together the sugar, cocoa powder, and chocolate, and stir in the melted margarine to make a sort of chunky chocolate paste. Add the almonds and stir well. Set aside.

🍀 Lightly grease twelve 4-ounce canning jars or 6 half-pint jars.

🍀 Lightly flour a work surface. Punch down the dough and turn out onto the surface. Roll out the dough into an approximately 9 x 13-inch rectangle. Spread the chocolate mixture over the dough, leaving a ½-inch border around the edge. The way you will roll it will depend on if you are making 12 small babkas or 6 larger ones. If you are making 12 small ones, start on the long edge and roll, making it a long, skinny roll. If you are making the larger rolls, roll it from the shorter edge, making a fatter roll.

🍀 For 12 small babkas, cut the dough in half. Cut each of those halves in half. Now divide each of the 4 segments into 3 slices. Place each roll into a prepared 4-ounce jar.

🍀 For 6 large babkas, cut the roll in half. Cut each of those halves into 3 slices and place each one into a lightly greased half-pint jar.

🍀 Place the jars on a rimmed baking sheet and cover with a dish towel. Allow the rolls to rise until they are about 1½ times the size they were when you started, about 45 minutes. Preheat the oven to 375°F and bake for 18 to 23 minutes for the small babkas or 23 to 27 minutes for the large ones, until golden and "blooming" in the jars.

🍮 Let cool on a wire rack for at least 20 minutes before serving.

# RASPBERRY MATCHA MUFFINS

Matcha is a green tea powder that adds a lovely flavor and green hue to everything it touches. These tender muffins are punctuated with bursts of tart raspberries for a delightful combination. Matcha powder can be very pricey by the jar or box, so check to see if your store offers teas in bulk; it's much more economical for smaller amounts.

## INGREDIENTS

1½ cups unbleached all-purpose flour

⅔ cup evaporated cane sugar

1 tablespoon matcha powder

½ teaspoon baking powder

⅛ teaspoon salt

¾ cup non-dairy milk of choice

½ teaspoon mild vinegar

¼ cup mild vegetable oil

1 cup fresh raspberries

coarse sugar, for sprinkling

**Makes 4 or 8 muffins**

## DIRECTIONS

🍃 Preheat the oven to 350°F. Lightly grease 4 half-pint or eight 4-ounce canning jars. Place the jars on a rimmed baking sheet.

🍃 In a small bowl, whisk together the flour, sugar, matcha, baking powder, and salt. In a large bowl, combine the milk, vinegar, and oil. Add the dry ingredients to the wet in two batches, mixing until just combined. Gently fold in the raspberries.

🍃 Fill each jar ⅔ of the way full with batter. Sprinkle the tops of each muffin with a little of the coarse sugar.

🍃 Bake for 23 to 26 minutes for large muffins and 16 to 20 for smaller muffins, until they are a darker green and a toothpick inserted in the middle of a muffin comes out clean. Let cool for at least 20 minutes before serving.

# SNICKERDOODLE PULL-APARTS

I love a good breakfast pastry. We name them as such so we can excuse having dessert upon waking. These adorable, individual pull-aparts bring a classic cookie to the table and they look absolutely charming. You can even prep them overnight, so they're fresh and yeasty the next morning. Soy or hemp milks are best for this recipe.

## INGREDIENTS

⅓ cup warm non-dairy milk of choice

1 (¼-ounce) packet active dry yeast

½ cup evaporated cane sugar, divided

6 tablespoons non-dairy margarine, melted, divided

⅓ teaspoon salt

2¼ cups unbleached all-purpose flour, plus additional for dusting

1 tablespoon ground cinnamon

**Makes 6 pull-aparts**

## DIRECTIONS

In a large bowl, place the milk, yeast, and 2 tablespoons of the sugar and let the yeast proof (become foamy) for about 5 minutes. Add 2 more tablespoons sugar and 4 tablespoons of the melted margarine and whisk. In a small bowl, mix the salt with the flour and begin to incorporate into the milk mixture, in two parts, until a soft dough comes together. Gently knead the dough on a floured surface until it is smooth and elastic, 5 to 7 minutes. Place it back in the bowl, cover with a dish towel, and let it rise until doubled in size, about 1½ hours.

Combine the remaining ¼ cup sugar and the cinnamon in a small bowl and set aside. Lightly grease 6 half-pint canning jars and set on a rimmed baking sheet.

Lightly flour a work surface. Punch down the dough and turn out onto the surface. Roll out the dough into an approximately 10 x 12-inch rectangle. Brush the top with the remaining 2 tablespoons melted margarine, then sprinkle the cinnamon-sugar mixture evenly over the top of the pastry. Using a pizza cutter or a sharp knife, cut the dough into 2-inch squares, creating 30 squares of dough. Stack them on top of each other, 5 slices high, to create 6 stacks of 5 slices. Carefully tip the stacks sideways and slide them into each prepared jar, like you are filing the slices of dough.

Cover with a towel and let them rise until doubled, about 45 minutes. Conversely, if you are making these the night before, cover with a dish towel and place in the fridge. Be sure to remove them from the fridge 1 hour before baking the next morning.

Preheat the oven to 375°F. Bake the pull-aparts for 23 to 27 minutes, until lightly browned and they are risen and are poking out of the jar tops. Let cool on a wire rack for at least 20 minutes before serving.

**NOTE:** You can make an optional glaze to drizzle over the top of the finished rolls by combining 1 tablespoon non-dairy milk with ⅓ to ½ cup powdered cane sugar. Whisk to combine and adjust to your preferred level of sweetness and thickness, then drizzle over the top of the pastries after they have slightly cooled.

# DATE AND WALNUT BREAD

Busting out your pint-sized canning jars will ensure you end up with two tender, moist loaves of bread, lightly sweetened and speckled with delicious chunks of dates and nuts. Plus, you can serve your friends and family round slices of bread—how fun is that?!

## INGREDIENTS

1½ cups unbleached all-purpose flour

⅓ cup evaporated cane sugar

1 teaspoon baking powder

½ teaspoon baking soda

½ teaspoon ground cinnamon or cardamom

⅛ teaspoon salt

1 cup non-dairy milk of choice

½ teaspoon mild vinegar

3 tablespoons mild vegetable oil

1 teaspoon vanilla extract

⅓ cup chopped pitted dates

⅓ cup chopped walnuts

**Makes two 1-pint loaves**

## DIRECTIONS

☛ Preheat the oven to 375°F. Lightly grease two 1-pint canning jars and place on a rimmed baking sheet.

☛ In a small bowl, whisk together the flour, sugar, baking powder, baking soda, cinnamon or cardamom, and salt. In a large bowl, combine the milk and vinegar. Whisk in the vegetable oil and vanilla. In two batches, incorporate the dry ingredients into the wet until just mixed. Gently fold in the dates and walnuts.

☛ Divide the batter between the 2 prepared jars. Bake for 27 to 32 minutes, until a toothpick inserted into a loaf comes out clean and the loaves are golden brown.

# COFFEE CAKES

I can think of no better way to earn the affections of your coworkers than to gift them with lovely little jars of coffee cake. When the work is piling up, a little sumthin' sumthin' with their morning coffee is sure to save a week on the brink.

## INGREDIENTS

**TOPPING:**

⅓ cup plus 2 tablespoons evaporated cane sugar

1 teaspoon ground cinnamon

dash of freshly grated nutmeg

4 tablespoons (¼ cup) melted non-dairy margarine

⅔ cup unbleached all-purpose flour

**CAKE:**

1½ cups unbleached all-purpose flour

⅔ cup evaporated cane sugar

½ teaspoon baking powder

½ teaspoon ground cinnamon

⅛ teaspoon salt

¾ cup non-dairy milk of choice

½ teaspoon mild vinegar

3 tablespoons mild vegetable oil

1 teaspoon vanilla extract

**Makes 4 or 8 cakes**

## DIRECTIONS

🍂 Preheat the oven to 350°F. Lightly grease 4 half-pint or eight 4-ounce canning jars. Place the jars on a rimmed baking sheet.

🍂 To make the topping, combine the sugar, cinnamon, and nutmeg in a small bowl. Add the melted margarine and stir until creamy. Use a pastry blender or the back of a strong fork to work in the flour until combined and it looks and feels like wet sand. Refrigerate.

🍂 For the cake, combine the flour, sugar, baking powder, cinnamon, and salt in a small bowl. In a large bowl, whisk together the milk, vinegar, oil, and vanilla. Add the dry ingredients to the wet in two batches, mixing until just combined.

🍂 Fill each jar ⅔ of the way full. Retrieve the topping from the fridge and divide the crumble among the jars, pressing it down lightly. Bake for 25 to 28 minutes for large cakes and 18 to 23 for smaller cakes, until they are golden and a toothpick inserted in the middle of a cake comes out clean.

🍂 Let cool on a wire rack for 20 minutes before serving.

# ZUCCHINI APPLE BREAD

Zucchini bread is always a winner and a great way to absorb an abundance of the little green squash we all find ourselves with in the summer. But the addition of dried apples, toothsome and intensely flavored, perks up this classic. If you'd like, raisins can easily sub for the apples, or you can take it in a totally different direction with chopped dates or dried cranberries. This is a flexible recipe.

## INGREDIENTS

1½ cups unbleached all-purpose flour

½ cup quick-cooking oats

¾ cup evaporated cane sugar

1 teaspoon baking powder

½ teaspoon baking soda

½ teaspoon ground cinnamon

⅛ teaspoon salt

¾ plus 2 tablespoons non-dairy milk of choice

½ teaspoon mild vinegar

⅓ cup mild vegetable oil

1 teaspoon vanilla extract

1 cup shredded zucchini

¾ cup chopped dried apples

**Makes three 1-pint loaves**

## DIRECTIONS

🍤 Preheat the oven to 350°F. Lightly grease three 1-pint jars. Place the jars on a rimmed baking sheet.

🍤 In a medium bowl, whisk together the flour, oats, sugar, baking powder, baking soda, cinnamon, and salt. In a large bowl, whisk together the milk, vinegar, oil, and vanilla. Incorporate the dry ingredients into the wet in batches, until just combined. Gently fold in the zucchini and dried apple chunks until just incorporated.

🍤 Fill each jar ¾ full and bake for 28 to 35 minutes, or until golden and a toothpick inserted into a loaf comes out clean. Let the bread cool on a rack before serving.

# CHAPTER 5

# Odds and Ends

"Odds and Ends" is a nice catchall for the moist crumbs and sweet bites that defy categorization. Kicking and screaming, we force them into this category where they learn to live peacefully and to respect their culinary diversity.

# ANISE DONUTS WITH ORANGE CREAM

Anise is a favorite old-world flavor of mine. It transports me to my grandma's kitchen, where I would eat anise cookies while she gossiped in Polish on the phone with her friends. As an adult, I encountered the French gibassier, an anise donut of sorts, speckled with candied orange, and was delighted to see my beloved, underrepresented anise in a pastry. This is my own twist on that, a tender baked donut, piped with a creamy orange filling. Soy or hemp milks are best for this recipe, as they have higher fat contents than some other non-dairy milks.

## INGREDIENTS

1 cup unbleached all-purpose flour

½ cup plus 2 tablespoons evaporated cane sugar, divided

1½ teaspoons baking powder

⅛ teaspoon salt

½ teaspoon ground anise seed or ¼ teaspoon anise extract

½ cup non-dairy milk of choice

½ teaspoon mild vinegar

¼ cup non-dairy margarine, melted

1 recipe Orange Cream Filling (page 112)

**Makes 6 donuts**

## DIRECTIONS

Preheat the oven to 350°F. Lightly grease and flour six 4-ounce canning jars. Place on rimmed baking sheet and set aside.

In a small bowl, combine the flour, ½ cup of the sugar, and the baking powder, salt, and anise seed (if using extract, reserve). Whisk to combine. In a larger bowl, whisk the milk and vinegar to combine. Whisk in the margarine and anise extract, if using. In two batches, incorporate the wet ingredients into the dry until just mixed.

Divide the batter evenly among the jars. Bake for 14 to 17 minutes, until a toothpick comes out clean. Let them cool completely on a rack.

While the donuts are baking, prepare the Orange Cream and refrigerate. Once the donuts are cooled, spoon the cold Orange Cream into a pastry bag fitted with a large tip. Insert the tip into the middle of each donut and gently pump the filling inside, watching until they gently rise. Remove the tip before rupturing the donut and repeat. Top each donut with 1 teaspoon of the reserved sugar to coat the top.

# RASPBERRY BROWNIE BOMBS

Rich, fudgy brownies topped with tangy raspberry cream. If you find yourself sleep-eating these at 3 a.m.—sprawled out in your kitchen, pajamas askew, lit by the fridge door you left ajar in haste— don't say I didn't warn you!

## INGREDIENTS

¾ cup unbleached all-purpose flour

½ cup evaporated cane sugar

¼ cup unsweetened baking cocoa, sifted

1 teaspoon baking powder

⅛ teaspoon salt

¼ cup non-dairy margarine, melted

⅓ cup non-dairy milk of choice, at room temperature

½ teaspoon vanilla extract

¼ cup non-dairy semisweet chocolate chips

1 recipe Raspberry Cream (page 114)

½ cup fresh raspberries

**Makes 6 brownie bombs**

## DIRECTIONS

🍫 Preheat the oven to 375°F. Lightly grease six 4-ounce canning jars and place on a rimmed baking sheet.

🍫 In a small bowl, whisk together the flour, sugar, cocoa, baking powder, and salt. In a large bowl, whisk together the melted margarine, milk, and vanilla. In two batches, combine the wet ingredients with the dry. Add the chocolate chips and stir until combined.

🍫 Divide the batter and fill each jar ⅓ full, smoothing the batter to level it out. Bake for 15 to 18 minutes, until the brownies are puffy and a toothpick inserted into a brownie comes out with moist crumbs, but not batter. Let cool completely on a cooling rack.

🍫 While the brownies are cooking, prepare the Raspberry Cream.

🍫 To serve, divide the fresh raspberries among the jars and place them on top of the brownies, in the center. Top each one with a large dollop of Raspberry Cream.

# PUMPKIN CRÈME BRÛLÉE

**Creamy, spiced pumpkin with a crisp sugar crust is as elegant as it is comforting.**

## INGREDIENTS

¾ cup non-dairy milk of choice

½ cup raw cashews

¾ cup plus 2 tablespoons evaporated cane sugar, divided

1 (15-ounce) can pumpkin purée (not pumpkin pie mix)

¼ cup maple syrup

1 teaspoon vanilla extract

1 teaspoon ground cinnamon

¼ teaspoon freshly grated nutmeg

¼ teaspoon ground ginger

⅛ teaspoon salt

**Makes 6 crème brûlées**

## DIRECTIONS

🍂 Set aside six 4-ounce canning jars

🍂 In a small bowl, combine the milk and cashews. Let them soak for about 30 minutes. Place the milk and cashews in a food processor or blender container. Purée until creamy. Add ½ cup of the sugar and the remaining ingredients, and blend until creamy, scraping down the sides as needed, about 2 minutes.

🍂 Pour the pumpkin mixture into a saucepan over medium heat, stirring often, until it begins to bubble and thicken, about 5 minutes. Fill each jar to just under the brim, leaving about ¼ inch of space. Refrigerate the jars until ready the serve.

🍂 Just before serving, sprinkle 1 tablespoon of the remaining sugar over the top of each jar. There are two options for brûléeing the desserts: using a propane brûlée torch or by broiling the tops of the desserts. If using a torch, follow the manufacturer's instructions. If broiling, place the jars on a rimmed baking sheet and turn the broiler on high. Place the jars under the broiler, with about 2 inches of space between the jars and the element. Keeping a watchful eye (the sugar burns quickly), heat the jars until the sugar caramelizes and becomes brown, 30 seconds to 2 minutes, depending on the heat intensity.

**NOTE:** Don't feel like messing with the brûlée part of crème brûlée? This recipe is just as delicious as a lovely custard. Dollop some Coconut Whipped Cream (page 111) on top and call it good.

# CLASSIC CHEESECAKE CUPS

A cup of rich, creamy cheesecake. Cheesecake you can put a lid on and whip out anywhere you'd please. It's almost indecent.

## INGREDIENTS

### CRUST:

½ cup unbleached all-purpose flour

⅓ cup evaporated cane sugar

½ cup oats (quick-cooking or old-fashioned)

3 tablespoons plus 1 teaspoon cold non-dairy margarine or coconut oil

### CHEESECAKE:

1 (12.3-ounce) package silken tofu

1 (8-ounce) package non-dairy cream cheese

½ cup evaporated cane sugar

2 tablespoons maple syrup or agave nectar

1 tablespoon cornstarch

2 teaspoons fresh lemon juice

1 teaspoon vanilla extract

fresh fruit or preserves, for topping

**Makes 6 cakes**

## DIRECTIONS

🍲 Preheat the oven to 375°F. Lightly grease six 4-ounce canning jars. Place the jars in a baking pan with tall sides that are at least ¾ as high as the canning jars.

🍲 In a small bowl, prepare the crust. Combine the flour, sugar, and oats. Cut in the margarine or coconut oil using a pastry blender or the back of a fork. Divide the crust among the jars and press it into the bottoms.

🍲 Put a pot of water on the stove and bring it to a boil. While the water is heating, place the cheesecake ingredients in a food processor or a blender. Process until smooth, scraping down the sides as needed, about 2 minutes. Pour the filling into the jars, filling up to ½ inch from the top of each jar. Carefully pour the boiling water into the pan around the jars, being careful that the water doesn't go into the jars. Fill the pan so the water comes halfway up the sides of the jars.

🍲 Carefully place the pan in the oven and bake for 17 to 20 minutes, until the cheesecakes are golden on top but are still jiggly. Remove from the pan and cool completely on a rack. Refrigerate the cooled cheesecakes for at least 1 hour. Top with jam or fruit just before serving.

# BAKED PINEAPPLE PUDDING

**This pudding has a rich, creamy texture, punctuated with pineapple tang. It's comfort food at its finest, like the promise of sun on a cold winter's day.**

## INGREDIENTS

⅔ cup vanilla or plain non-dairy yogurt

⅓ cup evaporated cane sugar

2 tablespoons cornstarch

1 (8-ounce) can crushed pineapple with juice

2 tablespoons mild vegetable oil

1 teaspoon fresh lemon juice

½ teaspoon vanilla extract

**Makes 6 puddings**

## DIRECTIONS

🍠 Preheat the oven to 350°F. Lightly grease six 4-ounce canning jars. Place the jars in a baking pan with tall sides that are at least ¾ as high as the canning jars. Bring a large saucepan of water to a boil on the stovetop.

🍠 In a large bowl, whisk together the yogurt, sugar, and cornstarch until creamy. Incorporate the pineapple, vegetable oil, lemon juice, and vanilla. Whisk until combined.

🍠 Pour the filling into the jars, filling up to ½ inch from the top of each jar. Carefully pour the water into the pan around the jars, being careful that it doesn't go into the jars. Fill the pan so the water comes halfway up the sides of the jars.

🍠 Bake for 14 to 16 minutes, until the edges of the puddings are set, but the middles are still jiggly. Let them cool for 15 minutes before removing from the water bath. Let cool on a wire rack an additional 15 minutes before serving.

# CINNAMON RAISIN BAGEL PUDDING

I'm notoriously bad for buying more bagels than I can eat before they become unpleasantly hard and chewy. Thankfully, I love bread pudding, so this recipe allows me to use up those extra bagels in a most delicious way. These are lovely served with Custard Sauce (page 107) drizzled on top.

## INGREDIENTS

⅔ cup evaporated cane sugar, divided

2 teaspoons ground cinnamon

1 teaspoon cornstarch

2 cups non-dairy milk of choice

2 tablespoons maple syrup

1 teaspoon vanilla extract

4 cups cubed cinnamon raisin bagels, in 1-inch cubes (about 5 large bagels)

**Makes 6 puddings**

## DIRECTIONS

🍮 Preheat the oven to 350°F. Lightly grease six 4-ounce canning jars. Place the jars on a rimmed baking sheet.

🍮 In a small bowl, combine 3 tablespoons of sugar and the cinnamon. Coat the inside of the jars with a thin layer of the cinnamon-sugar. Set the extra cinnamon-sugar aside.

🍮 In a large bowl, whisk together ⅓ cup of the sugar and the cornstarch until any clumps are broken up. Add the milk, maple syrup, and vanilla, and whisk to combine. Stir in the bagel chunks until they are well coated with the milk mixture. Let sit for 5 minutes.

🍮 Divide the bagel mixture among the prepared jars, filling them to the top. Sprinkle the remaining cinnamon-sugar on top of each jar. Bake for 17 to 22 minutes, until golden brown and the sides of the jars look a little bubbly.

🍮 Let cool on a rack for at least 20 minutes before serving. These are great fresh out of the oven, but make an excellent leftover breakfast as well.

# RASPBERRY CLAFOUTI

I consider a clafouti the card I hold in my back pocket. It comes together from virtually nothing and can be made in a flash. It's sweet enough to be a tasty dessert, but not so much that it can't hold its own at a brunch.

## INGREDIENTS

½ (12.3-ounce) package silken tofu

¼ cup evaporated cane sugar

¼ cup unbleached all-purpose flour or brown rice flour

1 teaspoon baking powder

¼ teaspoon salt

1 cup non-dairy milk of choice

1 teaspoon vanilla extract

1 cup fresh raspberries (can use frozen, but lightly thaw before using)

**Makes 6 clafoutis**

## DIRECTIONS

🍮 Preheat the oven to 375°F. Lightly grease six 4-ounce canning jars. Set them on a rimmed baking sheet and set aside.

🍮 In a food processor, process silken tofu and sugar until smooth. Add the flour, baking powder, salt, and half of the milk. Process until smooth. Add the remaining milk and the vanilla, and process until incorporated.

🍮 Pour the batter evenly among the prepared jars and sprinkle raspberries evenly on top. Bake for 15 to 18 minutes, until the edges are set and middle is still a little jiggly. Let cool on cooling rack at least 20 minutes before serving. Best served warm. Store leftover clafoutis covered in the fridge.

# CHAPTER 6

# Treats for Two

We don't always need a whole cake or two dozen cookies. We don't always have time to mess with it and to get it together. In those moments, these treats for two come to the rescue, providing emergency (portion-controlled) dessert relief.

# BASIC VANILLA CAKE FOR TWO

Sometimes you just need to bring it back to the basics.

## INGREDIENTS

3 tablespoons evaporated cane sugar

1 tablespoon plus 1 teaspoon mild vegetable oil

3 tablespoons non-dairy milk of choice mixed with ⅛ teaspoon mild vinegar

½ teaspoon vanilla extract

¼ cup unbleached all-purpose flour

¼ teaspoon baking soda

sprinkle of salt

Topping of your choice: jam, Hot Fudge Sauce (page 110), a scoop of ice cream...

**Makes 2 cakes**

## DIRECTIONS

🍃 Preheat the oven to 350°F. Lightly grease and flour 2 half-pint canning jars and place on a rimmed baking sheet.

🍃 In a small bowl, combine the sugar and oil and whisk until well combined. Add the milk (mixed with vinegar) and the vanilla extract, and whisk until smooth. Add the flour, baking soda, and salt, and whisk until just combined.

🍃 Divide between the 2 prepared jars and bake for 10 to 14 minutes, until golden and a toothpick inserted into the center of a cake comes out clean.

🍃 Let cool for at least 20 minutes before crowning with a topping and serving.

# CHOCOLATE CAKE FOR TWO

Chocolate cake is an open canvas with endless topping options. Whatever you have lying around, it will be perfect here.

## INGREDIENTS

¼ cup unbleached all-purpose flour

3 tablespoons evaporated cane sugar

2½ tablespoons unsweetened baking cocoa powder, sifted

¼ teaspoon baking soda

¼ cup plus 1 tablespoon non-dairy milk of choice

1 tablespoon plus 1 teaspoon mild vegetable oil

¼ teaspoon vanilla extract

1 tablespoon chopped non-dairy semisweet chocolate chips

Topping of your choice: jam, a dollop of Coconut Cream (page 111), fresh fruit...

**Makes 2 cakes**

## DIRECTIONS

🍫 Preheat the oven to 350°F. Lightly grease and flour 2 half-pint canning jars and place on a rimmed baking sheet.

🍫 In a small bowl, whisk together the flour, sugar, cocoa powder, and baking soda. Make a small well in the middle of the dry mixture and add the milk, oil, and vanilla. Mix until just combined then gently add the chocolate chips.

🍫 Divide between the 2 prepared jars and bake for 10 to 14 minutes, until a toothpick inserted into a cake comes out clean. Let cool on a wire rack for at least 20 minutes before topping and serving.

# BLUEBERRY BREAKFAST MUFFINS FOR TWO

Here's a tasty breakfast on the go. Just screw on the lid and you're out the door with a fresh blueberry muffin at your side.

## INGREDIENTS

¼ cup unbleached all-purpose flour

2 tablespoons quick-cooking oats

2 teaspoons evaporated cane sugar

⅛ teaspoon ground cinnamon

¼ teaspoon baking powder

sprinkle of salt

¼ cup non-dairy milk of choice mixed with ⅛ teaspoon mild vinegar

1 tablespoon plus 1 teaspoon mild vegetable oil

¼ teaspoon vanilla extract

3 tablespoons fresh blueberries

Makes 2 muffins

## DIRECTIONS

🍮 Preheat the oven to 350°F. Lightly grease and flour 2 half-pint canning jars and place on a rimmed baking sheet.

🍮 In a small bowl, whisk together the flour, oats, sugar, cinnamon, baking powder, and salt. Make a well in the middle and add the milk (mixed with vinegar), oil, and vanilla. Stir until just combined and gently fold in the blueberries.

🍮 Divide the batter between the 2 jars and bake for 15 to 19 minutes, until golden and a toothpick inserted in the center comes out clean.

🍮 Let cool on a wire rack for 20 minutes before serving.

# PB BANANA CAKE FOR TWO

**Need dessert? Have a lonely banana sitting around? Here's your answer.**

## INGREDIENTS

¼ cup unbleached all-purpose flour

3 tablespoons evaporated cane sugar

¼ teaspoon baking powder

3 tablespoons natural creamy peanut butter

¼ cup non-dairy milk of choice

2 tablespoons mild vegetable oil

1 large banana, half mashed, half sliced into half moons

**Makes 2 cakes**

## DIRECTIONS

🍠 Preheat the oven to 350°F. Lightly grease 2 half-pint canning jars and set on a rimmed baking sheet.

🍠 In a small bowl, whisk together the flour, sugar, and baking powder. In another bowl, combine the peanut butter, milk, and oil and stir until creamy. Mix in the mashed half of the banana. In two batches, add the dry ingredients to the wet until just mixed. Gently fold in the banana slices.

🍠 Divide the batter between the 2 jars and bake for 12 to 16 minutes, until golden and a toothpick inserted in the center comes out free of batter (it might be moist from the bananas; that's okay).

🍠 Let the cakes cool on a wire rack for 15 minutes before serving.

# DOUBLE THE PLEASURE COOKIE JAR

A dozen cookies can be too much of a temptation, so avoid succumbing to the inevitable with these tasty jars, bursting with just enough to satisfy your inner Cookie Monster.

## INGREDIENTS

1 tablespoon plus 1 teaspoon non-dairy margarine, melted

3 tablespoons packed brown sugar

¼ teaspoon vanilla extract

⅓ cup unbleached all-purpose flour

⅛ teaspoon baking powder

sprinkle of salt

3 tablespoons non-dairy semisweet chocolate chips

non-dairy ice cream, for topping (optional)

**Makes 2 cookies**

## DIRECTIONS

🍪 Preheat the oven to 350°F. Lightly grease two 4-ounce canning jars and set on a rimmed baking sheet.

🍪 In a small bowl, stir together the melted margarine, brown sugar, and vanilla until creamy. Add the flour, baking powder, and salt and mix until combined. Add the chocolate chips.

🍪 Divide between the 2 prepared jars and press down into the bottom firmly. Bake for 6 to 10 minutes, until golden and the edges are set. Let cool on a wire rack for 10 minutes before topping with a healthy scoop of ice cream and devouring.

# CHAPTER 7

# Mixes

If you can't surprise someone with the finished product, you can still gift a lovely jar filled with a dry mix. Doll it up with a ribbon and the instructions for sealing the deal and you can still feel good that you're baking for your loved ones.

# BROWNIE MIX

You know those moments when you're out of, like, everything and desperately wish you had enough flour to scrape together a treat, but going to the store just isn't going to happen? Finding this jar of brownie mix in the cupboard will save the day when your loved ones find themselves stuck, treatless and in sweatpants.

## INGREDIENTS

1½ cups evaporated cane juice

1 cup unsweetened baking cocoa, sifted

2 cups unbleached all-purpose flour

1 teaspoon baking soda

¼ teaspoon salt

⅓ cup non-dairy semisweet chocolate chips

## DIRECTIONS

🍫 Combine the sugar and baking cocoa in the bottom of a 1-quart canning jar. Swirl to combine, then press down with the back of a spoon. Wipe down the sides of the jar so the cocoa dust doesn't obscure the other ingredients. Layer the remaining ingredients as listed. Gently tap the jar between layers to settle. Top with lid and a tag with directions:

## VEGAN BROWNIES

### Makes 16 large, fudgy brownies

🍫 Preheat the oven to 350°F. Lightly grease and flour an 8 x 8-inch pan or line with parchment paper.

🍫 In a large bowl, empty out the jar contents and mix well. In a smaller bowl, combine the following:

⅔ cup non-dairy milk of choice

½ cup mild vegetable oil

1 teaspoon vanilla extract

½ teaspoon mild vinegar

🍫 Make a well in the middle of the dry ingredients and add the wet, mixing until just combined. Pour the batter into the prepared pan. Bake for 30 to 35 minutes, until the edges are set and a toothpick inserted in the center comes out with your desired level of fudginess.

🍫 Let cool on a cooling rack for at least 1 hour before cutting and serving.

# CRANBERRY QUICK BREAD MIX

**Cranberry quick bread is a cold weather necessity.**

## INGREDIENTS

1½ cups unbleached all-purpose flour

2 teaspoons baking powder

½ teaspoon baking soda

¼ teaspoon salt

½ cup evaporated cane sugar

1 cup quick-cooking oats

⅓ cup chopped walnuts or pecans

½ cup dried cranberries

## DIRECTIONS

Combine the flour, baking powder, baking soda, and salt in the bottom of a 1-quart canning jar. Swirl to combine, then press down with the back of a spoon. Layer the remaining ingredients as listed. You can adjust the amount of nuts and cranberries to fill the jar. Gently tap the jar between layers to settle. Top with lid and a tag with directions:

### CRANBERRY QUICK BREAD

**Makes 1 loaf, about 12 slices**

Preheat the oven to 375°F. Lightly grease a standard 9 x 5-inch loaf pan. Pour out the jar contents into a large bowl and stir to combine.

In a separate bowl, stir together:

1¼ cups non-dairy milk of choice

⅓ cup mild vegetable oil

1 teaspoon vanilla extract

½ teaspoon mild vinegar

Create a well in the dry ingredients and add the wet ingredients. Mix until just combined. Spread the batter into the prepared loaf pan. Bake for 45 to 50 minutes, until golden and a toothpick inserted in the center comes out clean. Let the bread cool completely on a rack.

# CHERRY ALMOND SCONE MIX

Scones tend to be overlooked in the baking-mix world, but they are great for filling those pint-sized jars and provide a perfect breakfast for your loved ones.

## INGREDIENTS

1½ cups unbleached all-purpose flour

2 tablespoons baking powder

¼ teaspoon salt

¼ cup evaporated cane sugar

⅓ cup dried cherries

¼ cup sliced almonds

## DIRECTIONS

🥄 Combine the flour, baking powder, and salt in the bottom of a 1-pint canning jar. Swirl to combine, then press down with the back of a spoon. Layer the remaining ingredients as listed. Gently tap the jar between layers to settle. Top with lid and a tag with directions:

### CHERRY ALMOND SCONES

**Makes 8 scones**

🥄 Preheat the oven to 400°F. Lightly grease an 8-inch round pan. Empty the contents of this jar into a bowl. Cut ¼ cup of cold non-dairy margarine into the flour mixture, until it becomes a crumbly meal.

🥄 In a small bowl, combine ½ cup plus 2 teaspoons non-dairy milk of choice with ½ teaspoon mild vinegar. Stir to combine and then add to the dry meal, mixing just until a nice dough comes together. Spread into the prepared pan and gently score the scones into 8 wedges.

🥄 Bake for 20 to 25 minutes, until golden and a toothpick inserted into a scone comes out clean. Let the scones cool on a cooling rack for at least 20 minutes before serving.

# COWGIRL COOKIES MIX

**These cookies have everything you need: peanuts, chocolate, and oatmeal.**

## INGREDIENTS

1⅓ cups unbleached all-purpose flour

1½ teaspoons baking powder

1 teaspoon baking soda

¼ teaspoon salt

1 cup evaporated cane sugar

1 cup quick-cooking oats

¾ cup non-dairy semisweet chocolate chips

⅓ to ¼ cup halved roasted peanuts

## DIRECTIONS

🌵 Combine the flour, baking powder, baking soda, and salt in the bottom of a 1-quart canning jar. Swirl to mix. Press down with the back of a spoon to settle, then top with the sugar and oats, in 2 distinct layers. You can gently rap the jar on a table to help settle the layers. Top with the chocolate chips and peanuts to fill the jar. Top with lid and a tag with directions:

---

# COWGIRL COOKIES

**Makes 2 dozen cookies**

🌵 Preheat the oven to 350°F and line a cookie sheet with parchment paper. Pour the jar contents into a large bowl and stir to combine.

🌵 In a smaller bowl, stir together:

> ¾ cup non-dairy margarine, melted
>
> ½ cup creamy, natural peanut butter
>
> 1 teaspoon vanilla extract

🌵 Create a well in the center of the dry ingredients and add the peanut butter mixture, and mix to combine. You might need to use a strong spatula or just use your hands.

🌵 Scoop out cookie dough into large tablespoon balls onto the prepared cookie sheet. Flatten slightly and arrange 1 inch apart. Bake for about 10 minutes, until lightly browned and the edges are set. Let the cookies cool on the cookie sheet for 15 minutes before transferring to a cooling rack.

# ORANGE CREAMSICLE COOKIE MIX

Orange and vanilla like nothing before. This particular mix looks lovely if you layer 1 cup of flour, then the sugar, then the remaining flour for some contrast.

## INGREDIENTS

2 cups unbleached all-purpose flour

½ teaspoon baking powder

2 teaspoons baking soda

¼ teaspoon salt

1 cup evaporated cane sugar

½ cup non-dairy white chocolate chips

## DIRECTIONS

Combine the flour, baking powder, baking soda, and salt in the bottom of a 1-quart canning jar. Swirl to mix. Press down with the back of a spoon to settle, then top with the sugar, then the chocolate chips. You can gently rap the jar on a table to help settle the layers. Top with lid and a tag with directions:

## ORANGE CREAMSICLE COOKIES

### Makes 2 dozen cookies

Preheat the oven to 350°F and line a cookie sheet with parchment paper. Pour the jar contents into a large bowl and stir to combine.

Create a well in the center of the dry ingredient bowl and add:

> 1 cup non-dairy margarine, melted and cooled
>
> zest of 1 orange
>
> ¼ cup fresh orange juice
>
> 2 teaspoons vanilla extract

Mix to combine. You might need to use a strong spatula or just use your hands.

Scoop out the cookie dough into large tablespoon-size balls onto the prepared cookie sheet. Flatten slightly and arrange 1 inch apart. Bake for about 8 minutes, until lightly browned and the edges are set. Let the cookies cool on the cookie sheet for 15 minutes before transferring to a cooling rack.

# CHAPTER 8

# Jam on It!

Hot water bath canning can seem overwhelming, but it just requires some advance prep work. Be sure to have everything set out and read through the recipe completely first and you'll be just fine. If you're still uncertain about the water bath, though, you can always make freezer jam, which is very simple. You can find freezer jam jars in the same area of the store where the glass canning jars are stocked.

# APPLE PIE BUTTER

**Richly spiced, creamy apple pie butter makes everything better. Spread it on bread or scones or biscuits. Add a dollop to some smoked tofu with dinner. Seriously, it's got your back.**

## INGREDIENTS

4 pounds apples, assorted varieties

2½ cups dark evaporated cane sugar

2 tablespoons fresh lemon juice

1 tablespoon plus 1 teaspoon ground cinnamon

1 tablespoon plus 1 teaspoon ground ginger

1 teaspoon freshly grated nutmeg

2 tablespoons pure vanilla extract

**Makes 4 half-pint jars**

## DIRECTIONS

- Prepare your canning jars, if canning in a hot water bath. Otherwise, prepare freezer jam jars and set aside.

- Peel and chop up all of the apples. You can also opt to peel them, roughly chop them, and then toss in the food processor to break them down a bit more. Place the apples in a large stockpot along with the sugar, lemon juice, cinnamon, ginger, and nutmeg, and mix well. Cook the apple mixture over medium heat until the juices are boiling and the apples become very soft and begin to break down, stirring often, 25 to 30 minutes.

- Process the apple mixture in a food mill, food processor, or blender in batches until it is creamy and smooth. Return to the pot, lower heat a bit, and add the vanilla. You may wish to add more sugar (do so ¼ cup at a time) or more spices, to taste. Be mindful that the spices will intensify after canning. Cook down until the mixture is thick and sticks well to a spatula or spoon, about 10 to 15 minutes more.

- Can according to manufacturer's directions in a hot water bath for 10 minutes. Remove the jars and let cool completely. Let the apple butter set for 24 hours before using.

# PLUM-BERRY JAM

Sweet plums and juicy berries give this jam a certain je ne sais quoi. Actually, the ingredients are below, so you do know what, but the complex flavor they create together will leave your friends and family guessing.

## INGREDIENTS

2 cups fresh plums, pitted and chopped

2 cups fresh blackberries

2 cups fresh blueberries

2⅔ cups evaporated cane sugar, divided

2 tablespoons fresh lemon juice

1 tablespoon powdered pectin

**Makes 4 half-pint jars**

## DIRECTIONS

🍏 Prepare your canning jars, if canning in a hot water bath. Otherwise, prepare freezer jam jars and set aside.

🍏 Combine the plums, blackberries, and blueberries in the bottom of a large stockpot. Add 2 cups of the sugar and the lemon juice, and cook over medium heat, stirring often. Once it comes to a simmer, gently crush up the fruit with a potato masher to your desired consistency. Remember that this is jam and not jelly, so chunks are acceptable.

🍏 Once the jam comes to a boil, combine the remaining ⅔ cup sugar with the pectin, and stir to break up any clumps. Add to the jam and stir well to combine. Lower the heat to medium and let the jam bubble and burp for 15 to 20 minutes, stirring continuously, until it begins to thicken.

🍏 Once the jam is thick and passes the "Gel Test" (see below), can according to the manufacturer's directions. Let it set up for at least 24 hours before using.

**GEL TEST:** The most important part of canning is to make sure your jam has a nice gel to it, ensuring it will be smooth and spreadable upon cooling. Check the gel of jam by placing a teaspoon of jam on a plate and putting it in the freezer for 1 minute. Push against the edge of the jam, and if it wrinkles up from the pressure of your finger, it is ready. It should actually slightly wrinkle, not smear. If not, let it cook for 3-minute intervals, checking the gel after each interval.

# STRAWBERRY RHUBARB JAM

This jam screams "spring is here!" One bite and you'll agree, even if your grass isn't quite there yet.

## INGREDIENTS

1½ pounds strawberries, hulled and chopped

1 pound rhubarb, chopped (add 1 more stalk if you want a bit more tang)

2 cups evaporated cane sugar

2 tablespoons plus 1 teaspoon lemon juice

2 tablespoons powdered pectin

**Makes 4 half-pint jars**

## DIRECTIONS

🖤 Prepare your canning jars, if canning in a hot water bath. Otherwise, prepare freezer jam jars and set aside.

🖤 Combine the strawberries, rhubarb, and sugar in a large bowl and let macerate for 1 hour. Transfer the mixture to a large stockpot, add the lemon juice and pectin, and bring to a boil over medium-high heat, about 20 minutes. Once boiling, mash with a potato masher until chunky. Lower the heat slightly and stir frequently, cooking until slightly reduced and thickened, 10 to 15 minutes.

🖤 Once the jam is thick and passes the "Gel Test" (page 99), can according to the manufacturer's directions. Let the jam set up for 24 hours before using.

# ORANGE AND APRICOT MARMALADE

The thing about marmalade is that it's tasty but can be unbearably bitter.
The thing about apricot jam is that it's tasty but can be unbearably sweet.
The two combine into a lovely spread that gives you the best of both worlds.
Navel oranges are fine here, but Valencia make it something really special.

## INGREDIENTS

4 large Valencia oranges

juice of 1 lemon

3 fresh apricots, pitted and chopped (skins left on)

¼ cup chopped dried apricots

4 cups water

2 cups evaporated cane sugar

**Makes 4 half-pint jars**

## DIRECTIONS

Prepare your canning jars, if canning in a hot water bath. Otherwise, prepare freezer jam jars and set aside.

Wash the oranges and cut off the hard ends, then cut half of the skin off of each orange, down to the flesh, and discard. Leave the remaining half of the skin on the oranges and slice into rounds as thin as you can make them. Then, roughly chop them and put in the bottom of a large stockpot. Add the remaining ingredients to the pot. Bring to a simmer and cook, with the lid off, for about 45 minutes. At this point, test the taste to make sure it's sweet enough for you. It should have some tang, but it should be pleasant. If needed, add another ¼ cup sugar.

Increase the heat to medium-high and bring to a boil. Cook for 10 more minutes, stirring constantly. Place a spoonful of the marmalade on a cold plate and chill in the freezer for 1 minute. It won't really wrinkle, but you should be able to tilt the plate around and the jam should stay thick and not be runny.

Can according to the manufacturer's directions. Let it set up for at least 24 hours before using.

# VANILLA BING JAM

Cherries with vanilla feels quite decadent. If you don't already own a cherry pitter, I'd recommend getting one. It makes quick work of preparing the cherries, and having such an esoteric kitchen gadget earns you serious street cred. A food processor makes chopping the cherries easy as pie (or jam).

## INGREDIENTS

4 pounds pitted Bing cherries (weighed after pitting), chopped

juice of 1 medium lemon

2 cups evaporated cane sugar

1 (1.75-ounce) box powdered pectin

2 large vanilla beans

**Makes 4 half-pint jars**

## DIRECTIONS

🍒 Prepare your canning jars, if canning in a hot water bath. Otherwise, prepare freezer jam jars and set aside.

🍒 Place the chopped cherries in the bottom of a large stockpot. Add the lemon juice. Cook over medium heat for 10 to 15 minutes, until the cherries begin to break down and release a lot of juice.

🍒 In a small bowl, combine sugar with the pectin and add to the cherries after the initial cook time. Combine well, stirring often, and bring to a low boil. Bring the mixture to a boil, and continue cooking until it begins to thicken, 15 to 20 minutes. Slice open the vanilla beans and scrape the seeds into the jam.

🍒 Once the jam is thick and passes the "Gel Test" (page 99), can according to the manufacturer's directions. Let the jam set up for at least 24 hours before using.

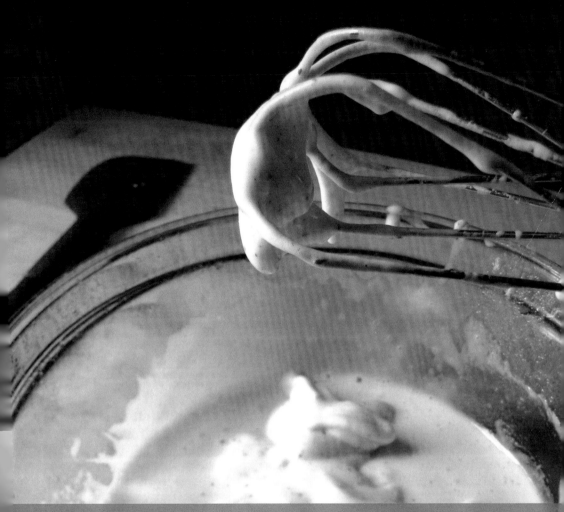

# CHAPTER 9

# Toppings and Fillings

Frostings and custards and sauces and drizzles, creamy piped fillings and hot fudge–doused vittles, berries and chocolate and nut butter creams, these are a few of my favorite things!

# BUTTERCREAM FROSTING

This frosting is creamy, simple, and classic. You can pipe it on top of pretty much anything and make it that much more delicious. For chocolate buttercream, simply add 3 tablespoons unsweetened baking cocoa, sifted, with the powdered sugar.

## INGREDIENTS

¾ cup non-dairy margarine, at room temperature

1½ to 2 cups powdered sugar, sifted

1 teaspoon vanilla extract

1 to 2 tablespoons non-dairy milk of choice (optional)

**Makes about 1 cup**

## DIRECTIONS

In a large bowl, cream the margarine until smooth. Add 1½ cups powdered sugar, adding up to ½ cup more to achieve the desired sweetness. Blend in the vanilla and as little of the milk, if using, as needed to make the frosting creamy and easy to spread.

Use the frosting immediately or store in the fridge for future use. If refrigerated, let it sit at room temperature for 20 minutes and stir well before using.

# CUSTARD SAUCE

This sauce is so simple and classic, you'll be pouring it on everything.

## INGREDIENTS

3 tablespoons evaporated cane sugar

1 tablespoon cornstarch

1 cup non-dairy milk of choice

1 tablespoon non-dairy margarine

½ teaspoon vanilla extract

**Makes 1 generous cup**

## DIRECTIONS

In a small saucepan, whisk together the sugar and cornstarch until there are no clumps. Slowly incorporate the milk and cook over medium heat, stirring constantly, until it comes to a light boil. Reduce the heat and cook, whisking continuously, until the sauce begins to thicken and coats the back of a spoon, about 3 minutes. Remove from the heat and whisk in the margarine and vanilla until smooth. Let cool for at least 20 minutes before serving.

# CREAMY CUSTARD

This tasty custard is incredibly versatile, which is exactly why it's utilized in a handful of different recipes. It's very creamy, lightly sweet, and goes with pretty much any treat. Soy or hemp milks are best for this recipe, as they have higher fat contents than some other non-dairy milks.

## INGREDIENTS

1½ tablespoons cornstarch

½ cup evaporated cane sugar

1½ cups non-dairy milk of choice

1 tablespoon non-dairy margarine

2 teaspoons vanilla extract

½ (12.3-ounce) package silken tofu

**Makes about 2 cups**

## DIRECTIONS

🥄 Whisk together the cornstarch and sugar in the bottom of a saucepan. Whisk in the milk and cook, whisking often, over medium-high heat, until it starts to bubble. Lower heat to medium-low and continue whisking until it begins to thicken and coats the back of a spoon. Remove from the heat, add the margarine and vanilla, and whisk to combine.

🥄 In a food processor or blender, blend the silken tofu until creamy. Carefully add the hot vanilla mixture to the tofu and blend until smooth, scraping down the sides as needed. Transfer to a heatproof bowl and refrigerate for at least 1 hour.

# CHOCOLATE GANACHE

This all-purpose spread doesn't need much of an introduction. It is fast and flexible—it's creamy, spreadable chocolate! I do offer this one note: I cannot take responsibility for any feuds which may arise over who gets to lick the bowl.

## INGREDIENTS

½ cup non-dairy chocolate chips or other chopped non-dairy chocolate

1 tablespoon non-dairy margarine or coconut oil

2 tablespoons non-dairy milk of choice

Makes ½ cup

## DIRECTIONS

To make it in the microwave: Combine all of the ingredients in a microwave-safe bowl. Microwave on high power in 10-second increments, stirring between each one, until the chocolate is melted and you can incorporate the other ingredients. It's important to stir even if it doesn't look like it needs it—chocolate burns easily.

To make it on the stovetop: In a double boiler or a heatproof bowl suspended over a pot with about 2 inches of simmering water in it, over medium heat, combine all of the ingredients and stir constantly until smooth. Be mindful that there is space between the bowl and the water; you want the hot steam to do the melting.

# HOT FUDGE SAUCE

You will undoubtedly find yourself pouring this sauce on everything. Don't worry, it's our little secret. Soy or hemp milks are best for this recipe, as they have higher fat contents than some other non-dairy milks.

## INGREDIENTS

3 tablespoons unsweetened baking cocoa

¼ cup brown evaporated cane sugar

2 tablespoons maple syrup or agave nectar

⅓ cup non-dairy milk of choice

½ cup non-dairy semisweet chocolate chips, divided

1 tablespoon non-dairy margarine or coconut oil

½ teaspoon vanilla extract

scant sprinkle of salt

**Makes about 1 cup**

## DIRECTIONS

In a small saucepan, combine the cocoa and brown sugar, whisking to break up any clumps. Add the maple syrup or agave and milk, and cook over medium heat, stirring frequently, until smooth and it begins to bubble. Add the chocolate chips and whisk to combine, reducing the heat to low. Once the chocolate chips are melted and incorporated, remove from the heat and stir in the margarine, vanilla, and salt. Combine well, then transfer to a heatproof container (a half-pint canning jar works great). Let cool for at least 20 minutes before using.

Fudge sauce should be refrigerated and will keep for 2 weeks in a covered container.

# COCONUT WHIPPED CREAM

This coconut whipped cream is deceptively simple and will change your life. Be sure that you use good old canned coconut milk, rather than the boxed coconut milk beverage, so the fat content is correct.

## INGREDIENTS

1 (14-ounce) can coconut milk (not low-fat)

½ teaspoon vanilla extract

¼ to ½ cup powdered sugar, sifted

Makes 2 cups

## DIRECTIONS

🍮 Refrigerate the coconut milk for at least 3 hours, overnight if possible. Open the can and scoop out only the hard, white coconut cream, leaving the watery part in the can. Place the coconut cream in a large bowl. Add the vanilla and ¼ cup powdered sugar. Using a stand mixer or electric hand mixer, whip the cream until fluffy. Add more powdered sugar, if necessary, to your desired sweetness.

🍮 Refrigerate for at least 2 hours before using. Store the coconut cream covered, in the fridge, for up to 4 days.

# CREAM CHEESE FILLING

This filling is delicious and creamy. You'll want to pipe it into everything you can get your hands on.

## INGREDIENTS

4 ounces non-dairy cream cheese

2 tablespoons non-dairy margarine, at room temperature

¾ to 1 cup powdered sugar, sifted

½ teaspoon vanilla extract

Makes a generous ½ cup

## DIRECTIONS

🍮 In a large bowl using an electric mixer on medium speed, beat together the cream cheese and margarine until combined. Add the powdered sugar, ¼ cup at a time, until the filling reaches your desired sweetness. Add the vanilla. Refrigerate the filling for 20 minutes before using, for best results.

# ORANGE CREAM FILLING

This filling can find its way into lots of tasty places, including but not limited to cakes, donuts, and brownies, or just let loose and plop it on top of some pancakes! Soy or hemp milks are best for this recipe, as they have higher fat contents than some other non-dairy milks.

## INGREDIENTS

1½ tablespoons cornstarch

½ cup evaporated cane sugar

1 cup non-dairy milk of choice

¼ cup fresh orange juice

2 teaspoons grated orange zest

1 tablespoon non-dairy margarine

1 teaspoon vanilla extract

½ (12.3-ounce) package silken tofu

**Makes 1 generous cup**

## DIRECTIONS

Whisk together the cornstarch and sugar in the bottom of a saucepan. Whisk in the milk and cook, whisking often, over medium-high heat, until it starts to bubble. Lower the heat to medium-low and continue whisking until it begins to thicken and coats the back of a spoon. Remove from the heat and add the orange juice, zest, margarine, and vanilla, and whisk to combine.

In a food processor or blender, blend the silken tofu until creamy. Carefully add the hot orange mixture to the tofu and blend until smooth, scraping down the sides as needed. Transfer to a heatproof bowl and refrigerate for at least 1 hour.

# BERRY SAUCE

**Simple, sweet, and saucy. Just the way it should be.**

| INGREDIENTS | DIRECTIONS |
|---|---|
| 4 cups fresh assorted berries (chopped strawberries, blueberries, chopped blackberries, raspberries)<br><br>¼ to ⅓ cup evaporated cane sugar<br><br>2 tablespoons water<br><br>¼ teaspoon fresh lemon juice<br><br>**Makes about ¾ cup** | ☛ In a large saucepan, combine the berries, ¼ cup sugar, water, and lemon juice. Whisk well and then bring to a boil over medium heat, stirring often. Lower the heat to a simmer. The berries should begin to burst and it will become very saucy. You can use the back of a large spoon or a potato masher to break up any large chunks of berries. If you aren't a fan of seeds, you can also push the sauce through a fine-mesh strainer to remove many of the seeds.<br><br>☛ Cook for an additional 3 to 5 minutes, until the sauce begins to thicken a bit. Taste for sweetness and add sugar, if necessary. Let the sauce cool before using. |

# PEANUT BUTTER FILLING

**Nom. Nom. Nom.**

| INGREDIENTS | DIRECTIONS |
|---|---|
| 4 ounces non-dairy cream cheese, at room temperature<br><br>⅓ cup natural creamy peanut butter<br><br>2 tablespoons non-dairy margarine, at room temperature<br><br>½ to 1 cup sifted powdered sugar, to taste<br><br>sprinkle of salt (optional, if using unsalted peanut butter)<br><br>**Makes about 1 cup** | ☛ In a medium bowl, use an electric hand mixer to combine the cream cheese, peanut butter, and margarine until smooth. Add the powdered sugar, starting with ½ cup and increasing the amount depending on the desired sweetness. Add the salt, if using. Mix until creamy.<br><br>☛ Store the filling in the fridge until using. Refrigeration might make it thicker, but a strong stir should make it nice and smooth. |

# RASPBERRY CREAM

Open mouth. Insert spoon of Raspberry Cream. Smile. Repeat. Making a double batch is never a bad idea.

## INGREDIENTS

½ (12.3-ounce) container silken tofu

½ cup frozen raspberries, thawed, with juices

¼ cup evaporated cane sugar

½ teaspoon vanilla extract

**Makes 1 heaping cup**

## DIRECTIONS

Combine the tofu, frozen raspberries, sugar, and vanilla in a food processor or blender, and purée until smooth and creamy, scraping down the bowl as needed. Spoon the cream into a container and refrigerate for at least 1 hour.

# MERINGUE TOPPING

This vegan meringue recipe would not exist had Miyoko Schinner not stretched the bounds of flaxseed goo further than one could ever dream possible. While this recipe may seem a little out there, rest assured that it will transform before your eyes from gelatinous goo to whipped and frothy meringue like magic. Before you feel too much like Harry Potter, do take note that this recipe takes a bit of prep work and you should wait to whip it up until right before serving. But what wouldn't you do to achieve the holy grail: vegan meringue!

## INGREDIENTS

⅓ cup flaxseed, golden or brown, 1 tablespoon of it ground

2 cups water

1 teaspoon agave nectar or maple syrup

⅛ teaspoon cream of tartar

2 to 4 tablespoons powdered sugar, sifted

**Makes 2 cups**

## DIRECTIONS

🥄 In a saucepan, combine the flaxseed and water. You want just a little of it ground to help increase the goo factor. Consequently, there might be some minor flecks of flax in your meringue, but it's a small price to pay. Bring the mixture to a boil over medium-high heat, then lower the heat to low and simmer for 15 to 20 minutes, until it gets really gooey and the mixture reduces by about half. Add the agave or maple syrup and stir to combine.

🥄 Pass the goo through a fine-mesh sieve or strainer to remove the seeds. You should have about ⅓ to ¾ cup of goo. Cool in a bowl and then transfer to the fridge, covered. Refrigerate for at least 1 hour, or up to 1 day.

🥄 While the goo is chilling, take a large bowl (not plastic—use metal or glass) and the beaters from your hand mixer and place in the freezer to chill. Alternatively, place the bowl and whisk beater from a stand mixer in the freezer. When ready to whip it up, transfer the goo to the cold bowl. Whip on high for 4 to 5 minutes, until it transforms from transparent goo into a luscious white froth. Once you've achieved soft peaks, add the cream of tartar and a little powdered sugar, starting with 1 tablespoon and increasing until the peaks become stiffer and hold their shape.

🥄 Spoon or pipe the meringue onto to the tops of your Lemon Meringue Pies (page 47) and serve immediately.

**NOTE:** The meringue whips up best when cold—the colder the better (short of being frozen). If possible, let the goo rest in the fridge for a couple of hours before preparing.

# CONVERSIONS

## COMMON EQUIVALENTS

1 gallon = 4 quarts = 8 pints = 16 cups =128 fluid ounces = 3.8 liters

1 quart = 2 pints = 4 cups = 32 ounces = .95 liter

1 pint = 2 cups = 16 ounces = 480 ml

1 cup = 8 ounces = 240 ml

¼ cup = 4 tablespoons = 12 teaspoons = 2 ounces = 60 ml

1 tablespoon = 3 teaspoons = ½ fluid ounce = 15 ml

## TEMPERATURE CONVERSIONS

| FAHRENHEIT (°F) | CELSIUS (°C) |
|---|---|
| 200°F | 95°C |
| 225°F | 110°C |
| 250°F | 120°C |
| 275°F | 135°C |
| 300°F | 150°C |
| 325°F | 165°C |
| 350°F | 175°C |
| 375°F | 190°C |
| 400°F | 200°C |
| 425°F | 220°C |
| 450°F | 230°C |
| 475°F | 245°C |

# VOLUME CONVERSIONS

| U.S. | U.S. EQUIVALENT | METRIC |
| --- | --- | --- |
| 1 tablespoon | ½ fluid ounce | 15 milliliters |
| 1 tablespoon | 2 fluid ounces | 60 milliliters |
| 1 cup | 3 fluid ounces | 90 milliliters |
| 1 pint | 4 fluid ounces | 120 milliliters |
| 1 quart | 5 fluid ounces | 150 milliliters |
| 1 liter | 6 fluid ounces | 180 milliliters |
| 1 ounce (dry) | 8 fluid ounces | 240 milliliters |
| 1 pound | 16 fluid ounces | 480 milliliters |

# WEIGHT

| U.S. | METRIC |
| --- | --- |
| ½ ounce | 15 grams |
| ½ ounce | 30 grams |
| ½ ounce | 60 grams |
| ¼ pound | 115 grams |
| ⅓ pound | 150 grams |
| ½ pound | 225 grams |
| ¾ pound | 350 grams |
| 1 pound | 450 grams |

# INDEX

# ABOUT THE AUTHOR

**KRIS HOLECHEK PETERS** is a vegan baker, blogger, and lover of all things delicious (especially if they involve chocolate and peanut butter). She is the author of *The 100 Best Vegan Baking Recipes*, *Have Your Cake and Vegan Too*, and *The I Love Trader Joe's Vegetarian Cookbook*, and is also the writer of www.nomnomnomblog.com. She lives with her cats in the Midwest, where she practices lots of yoga and hoards Bundt pans.